Exploring Justice: The Ten Commandments

—— VOLUME I ——

PRIORITIES

ANNE ROBERTSON

Unless otherwise indicated, Bible quotations in this book are from the New Revised Standard Version Bible, copyright © 1989 by the National Council of Churches of Christ in the U.S.A. Used by permission. All rights reserved.

One book, many voices

Massachusetts Bible Society
831 Beacon St. #324
Newton Center, MA 02459

Book design by Thomas Bergeron
www.thomasbergeron.com
Typeface: Garamond, Gill Sans

ISBN-13: 978-0-9907212-9-1
1st Edition

PHOTOGRAPHY CREDITS

Image #1 (p.30) Chapter 1, Syrian Refugee Island of Lesbos, Courtesy of Yannis Behrakis, Reuters, 2015; Image #2 (p.33) Chapter 1, Beloved Community, Courtesy of Syracuse Cultural Workers, www.syracuseculturalworkers.com; Image #3 (p.36) Chapter 2, Wizard of Oz Over the Rainbow, Courtesy of MGM Studios; Image #4 (p.39) Chapter 2, By Francis Helminski – Own work, CC BY-SA 4.0. Wikimedia Commons; Image #5 (p.42) Chapter 2, Snake Rod, Courtesy of https://tinyurl.com/y2meds9d; Image #6 (p.48) Chapter 2, Ken Cedeno, photographer / Reuters Pictures; Image #7 (p.52) Chapter 2, Wizard of Oz and Toto, Courtesy of MGM Studios, 1939; Image #8 (p.60) Chapter 2, War on Christmas Cartoon, Courtesy of Rob Tornoe; Image #9 (p.62) Chapter 2, Jonathan Bachman, Reuters Pictures; Image #10 (p.73) Chapter 3, Demarsico, Dick, photographer, https://www.loc.gov/item/2004670155; Image #11 (p.78) Chapter 3, Chalkboard Pledge 1975 Emerson High School OKC, Courtesy of OKCPS Emerson High School; Image #12 (p.87) Chapter 3, British Corps of Royal Marines, Courtesy of Don Troiani, 2015; Image #13 (p.94) Chapter 3, AP Photo/Marcio Jose Sanchez; Image #14 (p.97) Chapter 3, Colin Kaepernick Nike Ad, Courtesy of Nike, Inc.; Image #15 (p.107) Chapter 4, Statistical Source: Speth, James Gustave, "America: The Best Country in the World at Being Last – How Can We Change That?" Alternet, 1 March 2012, http://bit.ly/xtghAU; Image #16 (p.123) Chapter 4, Tom's Doubts, #14 by Saji George; Image #17 (p.132) Chapter 5, Freedom Fries, Courtesy of VICE Media, LLC; Image #18 (p.135) Chapter 5, For Love of God and Country, Courtesy of Anthem Community Church; Image #19 (p.144) Chapter 5, "False Advertising?" by Brendan Boughen, cartoonist. www.cartoonstock.com; Image #20 (p.147) Chapter 5, Stu's Views Law Cartoons, www.stus.com; Image #21 (p.158) Chapter 5, AP Photo / Jacquelyn Martin; Image #22 (p.162) Chapter 5, Stephen A. Schwartzman Building / Rare Books Division / New York Public Library; Image #23 (p.164) Chapter 5, By Martin Kraft, CC BY-SA 3.0, https://tinyurl.com/y3upf57g; Image #24 (p.165) Chapter 5, Silent Sam is Down, Courtesy of Samee Siddiqui, @ssiddiqui83; Image #25 (p.175) Chapter 6, Property of The Colonial Williamsburg Foundation, P.O. Box 1776, Williamsburg, VA 23187-1776;Image #26 (p.187) Chapter 6, AP Photo / Jim Cole; Image #27 (p.189) Chapter 6, Maria Butina with Gun, Courtesy of Maria Butina's Facebook Page; Image #28 (p.193) Chapter 6, Jon Shapley / © Houston Chronicle. Used with permission.; All other photos are public domain.

To Bill and Joan Humphrey
whose lives display
God's priorities at work in the world

CONTENTS

WELCOME

WHAT IS THIS EXACTLY?

You may know the Massachusetts Bible Society from our popular Bible study series, *Exploring the Bible: The Dickinson Series*. You may know me, Anne Robertson, for a variety of sermons and books on religion and the Bible. This book is both like and unlike what I've written in the past. The focus of this study series is on issues of justice in the public square. The Bible is the lens through which we are examining those issues, but, just as with reading glasses, the biblical lens will often fade into the periphery as it does its job of helping us see what's on the page. Here are a few important things to know before you dig in:

- **It's a series, designed to be read in order.** *Exploring Justice: The Ten Commandments* is a multi-volume series, and you are holding just one of its volumes. If this is your first encounter with this series and you're not looking at Volume 1, you will be at a disadvantage.

If this is your first encounter with this series and you're not looking at Volume 1, you will be at a disadvantage.

Starting with the command to have no other gods, each volume of *Exploring Justice* covers between one and three different commandments. The first volume establishes core themes that flow throughout the entire series, and each subsequent volume builds on that, just as the Ten Commandments themselves build on one another. Lightning will not strike if you do them out of order, but you will be quite likely to misunderstand or struggle. If you're joining a group that has already done another volume, at least pick up a copy of any volumes you may have missed and read the student book.

- **"Bible study" isn't exactly the right way to describe this series**. You will encounter the Bible in this study and, as the series title implies, the whole premise is that the Ten Commandments can help us keep today's social issues in conversation with the timeless values that inform our faith. You will also consider other passages from both the Old and New Testaments that relate to the themes of each chapter, and you'll be asked to think about their relevance to the issues at hand. In a typical Bible study, however, the object of study is the Bible itself, which is not the case here.

- **A Christian audience is assumed but not necessary**. Most of the people who do this study will be Christians in churches, but we ran a pilot group of humanists in a Unitarian congregation who also found it helpful. It's our hope that interfaith groups might also find the series useful for dialogue and understanding.

The Ten Commandments themselves are presented in the context of faith in the God of Abraham, Isaac, and Jacob, and they offer covenant relationship with that God. But, as a legal code, the commandments provide many points of connection to other religions as well as to contemporary, secular life. No matter our faith or lack thereof, we each have our own lens for viewing justice, and our own ideas of what values should be prioritized in society.

All of us will be looking at the teachings of the Bible and deciding whether the wisdom found there has anything to say to a given issue. Christians will have a different view of the authority of those teachings, but there's plenty of old-fashioned wisdom in the Bible that can shed light on our struggles, even for those who don't profess to "believe" it in the way that Christians do.

- **You can learn, even if everyone agrees.** This is a series about you, not those who disagree with you. It is designed to help you look inward at your own engagement with justice issues, not to encourage finger-pointing at those who reach different conclusions. While group discussions are enhanced by a diversity of people and opinions, there is much that we can learn about ourselves even within a group that is otherwise like-minded and from a similar background. This study will help you reflect not just on particular issues, but on the way we approach discussing those issues with others. It's possible to be "right" on any given issue and still violate our values in the way we approach others who hold a different position.

It's possible to be "right" on any given issue and still violate our values in the way we approach others who hold a different position.

- Jesus scolded those who tried to take a speck out of the eye of someone else while ignoring the logs in their own eyes, and this series tries to take that to heart. Bring a mirror to your study rather than one of those pointing foam fingers. If you look deeply and honestly into your own heart, you will also be much better equipped to handle any actual diversity in your group. You'll be so busy looking at the root of your own opinions and behavior that you'll be less likely to respond in a judgmental way to others.

Thank You for Supporting Us

Like our *Exploring the Bible* series, 100 percent of sales revenue from this series supports the mission of the historic Massachusetts Bible Society, a 501(c)3 charitable organization that exists to promote biblical literacy, understanding, and dialogue. You can learn more about the series and its other volumes by visiting us at massbible.org/exploring-justice. We are now in our third century, thanks to supporters who buy our books and/or make donations. If you'd like to help us even more, visit massbible.org/support-us.

CONFESSIONS OF A BIASED AUTHOR

Exploring Justice: The Ten Commandments wasn't written by a bot. It wasn't even written by a team of people. It was written by a single human—in this case, me. While I have done my best to be fair in presenting the issues, I have my own beliefs, ideas, and opinions about each topic in the book—just as every reader will—and it's probably a pipe dream to think that my own bias won't come through here and there.

So, I'll make a deal with you. As we go along, I'll poke my head out from time to time to share experiences or opinions on the subject at hand. I won't hide behind the voice of a supposedly impartial narrator, except when it comes to relating history or other factual information that you can look up and check yourself. You will know where I stand, which allows you to argue back in your group sessions instead of shadow boxing. In my own sharing, I'll try to model a way to express opinions and experiences that helps make real listening and dialogue possible. In return, I will ask that each of you do the same with your group, or, if you're just reading on your own, with whomever you choose to talk to about any of these issues. If you find I haven't done that, feel free to blast me in the evaluation at the end of this volume—tactfully, of course. Therapy is expensive.

I am the executive director of the Massachusetts Bible Society, and it's fair to say that they wouldn't publish this if they thought it was heresy. Both staff and board members were part of our pilot groups. But the opinions you'll find throughout these volumes are my own and have not received formal endorsement from the MBS board, members, or partner organizations. You can find the organization's official statement on Scripture at massbible.org/about-us/mission-statement.

THE TEN COMMANDMENTS: A BRIEF OVERVIEW

While each volume of the series will focus on different commandments, it's worth a bit of time to get a balcony overview of the Ten Commandments as a whole and to review their role in the biblical story. They are actually listed twice in the Bible: Exodus 20:1–17 and Deuteronomy 5:6–21. There are slight differences, which I'll highlight when relevant, but basically they are the same listing. Different faith traditions, however, look at the Ten Commandments in different ways, starting with the way they number them.

Exodus 34:28 says there are ten, so most numbering systems work with that, even though there are more than ten commands within the text. But since the Hebrew documents don't actually number the commandments, it's a guess exactly where each one begins and ends, and different traditions group them differently. Complicating the numbering process further is the fact that the Hebrew doesn't actually say the ten "commandments," but rather the ten "words." So, for example, "I am the Lord your God, who brought you out of the land of Egypt" in Exodus 20:1 is seen by the Jews as the first "word," even though it's not technically a commandment.

Even within Christian tradition there are different numbering systems. Roman Catholics and Lutherans, for example, combine the commandments about no other gods and graven images and then split up the coveting commandment into two: The coveting of people and the coveting of property. The default for this series is the system commonly used in most Protestant circles, which lays them out (in shortened form) this way. This text is from the King James Version of the Bible:

1. Thou shalt have no other gods before me.
2. Thou shalt not make unto thee any graven image.
3. Thou shalt not take the name of the Lord thy God in vain.
4. Remember the Sabbath day, to keep it holy.
5. Honor thy father and thy mother.
6. Thou shalt not kill.
7. Thou shalt not commit adultery.
8. Thou shalt not steal.
9. Thou shalt not bear false witness against thy neighbor.
10. Thou shalt not covet.

In the third century CE, a Rabbi named Simlai delivered a sermon that mentioned 613 commandments in the Torah (the first five books of the Bible). That has been Jewish tradition ever since. What's relevant for this series is that the Ten Commandments are seen by Jews as ten broad categories on which all the other commandments can be built. Those 613 commandments covered pretty much every life situation in ancient times—from aiding a donkey that has collapsed under its burden, to not eating a worm found in fruit, to treating parties in a litigation equally, and hundreds more. They cover sexuality, legal systems, labor laws, financial transactions, immigration status, worship practices, social interactions—you name it. And each of those very specific laws finds a place in Jewish teaching built on the foundation of the broad strokes of one of the Ten Commandments.

Since the Jews see the commandments as categories to provide guidance for all other laws and behaviors, I think it is worth the time for Christians, or even secular readers, to consider that model and to think about how these ten areas might help us explore the vexing problems we face as a society. As we progress through the volumes in this series, you'll see that these ten categories in no way limit the kinds of issues we can examine in their light.

The commandments in each volume are grouped under a common theme, which serves as the title for each volume. I have grouped the actual issues with the commandment(s) that seemed to give the most insight into the discussion, although in most cases a topic could have found a home under the banner of several different commandments. I've also steered the focus toward a social rather than an individual application. For example, the false witness commandment can spur all sorts of debate about whether an individual should ever tell a lie. Those are worthwhile conversations, but they will be secondary here. In this series, we'll be looking at the way we lie in our public life together, through institutions, policies, and our social contract with one another. I think that approach is true to the text.

THE PUBLIC SQUARE

The Ten Commandments weren't initially given to govern private behavior. They were the foundational principles for a new nation. They make up a constitution of sorts, offering a relationship with the God of Abraham, Isaac, and Jacob to all who would willingly place themselves under God's authority. Just as the United States Constitution doesn't govern people in other countries, so the Ten Commandments were not meant for other religions or nations. The Bible tells us that they were proposed to the Israelites, and the people were asked to accept or reject them. The commandments were not imposed without the consent of the people, but neither were the terms negotiable. There was no constitutional convention to hammer out exactly what commandments would be included. There's a reason for that.

By ordering life and law around the principles of the Ten Commandments, the new nation of Israel would bear public witness to the God they professed to serve and ensure that the vision of a just and peaceful society that God set forth could become a reality. If everyone abided by this new social code, they could move from the desert to a promised land that flowed with milk and honey. Everyone would have enough, because those who don't kill, steal, or covet; those who take care of the elders, make sure everyone has a day off, and put God's priorities first, will naturally look out for one another and not take more than they need. What a person did privately was important, but only because the system only works if everyone participates.

God didn't wake up one day and decide it would be fun to see if people could refrain from stealing. The commandments are not arbitrary demonstrations of God's power to declare certain behaviors right or wrong. Rather, they are the blueprint for a society that works for everyone, no matter where you fall on the social ladder. They are the vows to care for one another for better, for worse, for richer, for poorer, in sickness and in health. The Ten Commandments, ultimately, are about the intersection of individual behavior and public life— exactly where we find ourselves when confronted with the controversial issues of our day.

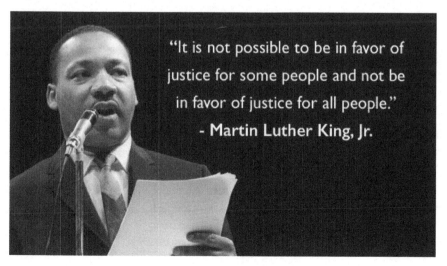

"It is not possible to be in favor of justice for some people and not be in favor of justice for all people."
- Martin Luther King, Jr.

WHY WE'RE HERE

The purpose of this series isn't to make public policy recommendations or to pronounce solutions to complex issues. The Ten Commandments weren't ever posted anywhere. God told Moses to put them in a box called the Ark of the Covenant and sit on them when he tried to figure out a fair solution to the specific problems people brought to him. The commandments didn't hold concrete answers for every problem; they were the outline of a broad, behavioral covenant. Moses had to think and pray and figure out how those principles applied in the thorny, day-to-day situations of the people. Sitting on them meant they were very literally the basis for his judgments, but nobody pretended that they were a how-to manual for every circumstance.

They will serve a similar role for us. People of goodwill can and do have legitimate differences on how problems are best solved. As we go about solving them, this series can help us keep our most fundamental values at the center of our debates about political and social issues.

People of goodwill can and do have legitimate differences on how problems are best solved. As we go about solving them, this series can help us keep our most fundamental values at the center of our debates about political and social issues.

The United States is not a theocracy, as ancient Israel was. Our Constitution forbids the establishment of a single national religion. However, saying that we don't (and can't) have a national religion as a matter of law is different than saying the faith and values of any individual should be put aside when engaging in public debate or making decisions that affect public life.

The Bible, in both Old and New Testaments, is clear about that. God didn't give commandments only about worship services or private life. God gave commandments about how to live together in society, in the public square. That's the larger meaning of politics—the word itself comes from the Greek word *polis*, which means "city." "Politics" actually means the art of living together in community. Where two or more are gathered, you have politics.

It's up to each of us, in conversation with the churches and other communities to which we belong, to determine our own relationship with God and to consider God's revelation to us, wherever our tradition finds it. On the basis of that, we must decide for ourselves how we'll live, how we'll vote, and how we'll engage the polis—our communities, cities, and nations. This series is designed to help us explore some of our most difficult issues together, hopefully without breaking the "thou shalt not kill" commandment in the process.

FEAR NOT

You might be a bit nervous in beginning this series. In our polarized society, even the most innocent of issues can hit a friendship like a lightning bolt. We've all seen difficult social problems tear at the fabric of families, churches, and nations. That's not how we want life to be. We want to have a place to ask our honest questions and express our concerns without fear of judgment or ridicule. We don't want every difference to become a divisive fissure, but sometimes it seems like we might fall into the abyss just by asking a question. Starting a group to talk about social issues in this climate seems risky, and a lot of us are happy to let someone else stand on the fault lines and work it out.

If that's you, you're in good company. That's how most of us feel when someone says, "Hey, let's have a group discussion about abortion. Won't that be fun?" When it comes to speaking our minds about difficult issues, often we'd rather just send the pastor or the bishop or someone—anyone—else to just work it all out and tell us about it later. Our concerns are real: What will happen if I say what I think? Suppose someone I care about has a different opinion and feels strongly about it? Will our relationship dissolve? What if my opinion differs from the formal teaching of my church? Suppose I share my experiences and they are met with ridicule or judgment instead of understanding?

Those tensions are as old as the Bible itself. A good chunk of the New Testament deals with clashes over differing interpretation of God's laws, culminating in Acts 15 in a full-blown council in Jerusalem over the issue of circumcision and whether Gentile believers in Jesus had to become Jews in order to join a Christian community. Many of Paul's letters indicate that there were tensions in the early churches over how to respond to specific cultural and social issues of the day. The leaders went toe-to-toe and then stepped back to explain their position and any decisions to the people. Those battles didn't erase the differences, but neither did they throw the majority of believers directly into the fight.

In that spirit, this series seeks to help all of you, both separately and together, to explore the hot, fiery issues of our day from a safe distance. We're not going to solve them or erase all differences, and we don't aim to try. But neither is anyone going to insist that you walk directly into the fire. We often think of social justice in terms of a fight. We talk about justice "warriors" and believe we need to be fierce in arguing for our position. There is a place for that. God is always calling some people to be on the front lines. But just like there are desk jobs in the armed services filled with people playing vital roles, so God calls many people to work for justice in ways that aren't quite so fraught.

This series is not the front lines. This is about education and dialogue and reflection. As the title implies, we are exploring justice. Our goal is to enable real dialogue and to provide a protected space to ask questions and think things through.

This series is not the front lines. This is about education and dialogue and reflection. As the title implies, we are exploring justice. Our goal is to enable real dialogue and to provide a protected space to ask questions and think things through.

Then, with a fuller understanding of both the issues and our own beliefs, we can listen for God's call to act in the role that we are uniquely gifted to fill. If just one group can learn to explore difficult issues without breathing smoke and fire, a seed of hope will be planted in the volcanic ash of our public discourse. Consider this: As of 2018 there were 2.5 billion Christians in the world, and it all started with one guy and his twelve disciples. That one guy is still with us. We can do this.

PRIORITIES

The Path to Justice

Social problems take a particular shape in each age and culture. Most of them, however, are rooted in deeper concerns that have been around since Adam and Eve first decided that fruit regulations needed to be relaxed. Underneath the thorniest social issues we typically find the struggles that have challenged human community since the get-go. How do we use power? How do we balance our needs with the needs of others? How do we manage conflict from within and without? What are our priorities and how do we navigate relationships with those whose priorities are different or even in competition with ours? As luck would have it, the Bible has wisdom and guidance for all of those fundamental human questions, assuring us that if we adopt God's priorities as our own, the promised land of peace, justice, and abundance will begin to emerge.

But we have to understand a few things before we can sign on to that offer. First, we have to figure out what God's priorities actually are and then ask ourselves a couple of things. Are those priorities truly our priorities? If everyone lived by them, would it bring about the world we want to have? And, finally, what does that ideal world actually look like? What are the characteristics that make it so perfect, and how can we acquire some of those attributes right now? Almost all of us would say that perfect world includes "justice." But what exactly is justice? What does it look like when it happens? Does "justice" mean every crook ends up in handcuffs, or is there something more?

These are the questions that define this chapter as we begin to explore justice in light of our highest values and beliefs.

WHAT DOES THE LORD REQUIRE?

As we saw in the Introduction, Judaism recognizes a whopping 613 commandments in the Hebrew Scriptures, and in the New Testament, many more are added for Christians. But are all commandments created equal? Most of us would be hard-pressed to believe that combining wool and linen (prohibited in Deuteronomy 22:11) is just as abhorrent to God as murder (forbidden in the sixth commandment) or that Paul's instruction that women shouldn't braid their hair (1 Timothy 2:9) is as important as the Golden Rule (Matthew 7:12). But is there some way for us to know which of the Bible's commands carry more weight? If we want to make God's priorities our priorities, where do we start? What does the Lord require of us? Can we have the CliffsNotes version, please?

I believe the Bible summarizes those priorities for us in three places: From God in the Ten Commandments, from Jesus in the Great Commandment, and from the Spirit of God through the prophet Micah. Yes, I overlaid the Trinity on my choices. Thanks for noticing.

Priority One: Be a Part of Something Bigger

There's an overview of the Ten Commandments in the Introduction that you should stop and read now if you haven't already. The main takeaways from that are two: First, these commands are a social code to ensure justice, peace, and abundance for all. Second, they constitute an offer from God that can be freely chosen or rejected. If you don't want to restrict yourself in the ways the Ten Commandments instruct, that's fine. You don't have to be part of the project. But, the clear message of God's offer is that there is something to be gained by becoming part of a larger community with shared values and practices.

Priority One: The Ten Commandments

- Thou shalt have no other gods before me.
- Thou shalt not make unto thee any graven image.
- Thou shalt not take the name of the Lord thy God in vain.
- Remember the Sabbath day, to keep it holy.
- Honor thy father and thy mother.
- Thou shalt not kill.
- Thou shalt not commit adultery.
- Thou shalt not steal.
- Thou shalt not bear false witness against thy neighbor.
- Thou shalt not covet.

We have to give up some individual freedoms to do that, but sacrificing to follow the code laid out in the Ten Commandments is what we give to attain the "promised land," not just for ourselves, but for everyone. To quote from the Introduction, in that land "everyone would have enough, because those who don't kill, steal, or covet; those who take care of the elders, make sure everyone has a day off, and put God's priorities first, will naturally look out for each other and not take more than they need." That end result is what biblical justice looks like, and nobody gets there by themselves. You have to buy the ticket and get on the bus with everyone else who wants to go there.

In giving the Ten Commandments priority over other laws in Scripture, we join Judaism, which sees these ten as the foundation on which all other laws are built. But can an ancient legal code from the Middle East still have relevance for us? Consider this: A clergy colleague recently told me that he was teaching a confirmation class and was stunned to learn that none of the kids in the class could name even one of the Ten Commandments. He could have sent them home to memorize them, but instead he asked the class to pretend that they were charged by God to make up the rules for the world. What would they be?

That group of adolescents, here in twenty-first-century Massachusetts, came up with seven of the Ten Commandments all on their own. That early social code and the issues it deals with are as relevant—and as vexing—as the morning news. Human culture has undergone enormous changes in the thousands of years since Israel accepted God's offer to let that code govern their lives. Human nature, however, has not changed one bit. The larger context may differ now, but their issues are still ours at their core, and it still takes all of us together to bring justice to the world.

Priority Two: Let the Test Be Love

The Ten Commandments turned into 613 for a reason. The Ten are broad categories with little guidance for the very particular messes we often find ourselves in. The classic example is the Sabbath commandment. Making one day in seven a day of rest is plain enough, but what does resting really mean? Do I have to sleep all day? Suppose I find gardening restful—can I do that? And how do we eat if someone has to work to cook the food?

With every new question, the law expanded to give more specific guidance to those who were trying to keep God's law but had trouble sorting out what it looked like in their own circumstance. And, of course, there were also those who were simply trying to find loopholes so they could earn more money or otherwise do what they wanted whenever they wanted. So laws were devised to cover those with less-than-pure motives, too.

By Jesus' day you had an entire profession of people, the Pharisees, whose job it was to interpret the law, just as today in the U.S. you can find a law firm on every corner. But getting your brain around it all was hard for the average person, and it got people asking if there was some broader guide that could be used from day to day without having to consult a lawyer just to eat breakfast. Wasn't there a way to, you know, sum it all up? A simple test to gauge whether God is pleased with what I'm doing?

Priority Two: The Great Commandment

"You" shall love the Lord your God with all your heart, and with all your soul, and with all your mind." This is the greatest and first commandment. And a second is like it: "You shall love your neighbor as yourself." On these two commandments hang all the law and the prophets. — Matthew 22:37–40

First-century lawyers liked to debate with Jesus, and in Matthew 22:35–40, one of them comes to Jesus with a test on this very issue: "Teacher, which commandment in the law is the greatest?" Notably, Jesus doesn't tell him they're all equally important. He doesn't even pick any of the Ten Commandments. Instead, he plucks out two other commandments, one from Deuteronomy 6:5 and the other from Leviticus 19:18, and strings them together:

"'You shall love the Lord your God with all your heart, and with all your soul, and with all your mind.' This is the greatest and first commandment. And a second is like it: 'You shall love your neighbor as yourself.' On these two commandments hang all the law and the prophets."

In Luke 10:25–37, there is a similar story, but there the lawyer doesn't ask what the greatest commandment is. Instead he asks, "What must I do to inherit eternal life?" The answer is the same, since the greatest commandment would naturally be the one that leads to eternal life.

But the lawyer in Luke wants more detail—and perhaps a loophole—in that broad command to love your neighbor as yourself. Surely Jesus can't mean, you know, *my* neighbor. So he asks, "And who is my neighbor?" With the parable of the Good Samaritan, Jesus squashes the implication that "neighbor" excludes anyone. Who is the neighbor? The one from the different religious and ethnic heritage who showed mercy. "Go and do likewise," Jesus tells the lawyer. Don't just love your neighbor; *be* a neighbor. Mr. Rogers, who was trained as a Presbyterian minister, built his "neighborhood" on solid biblical ground.

When we are sorting through the priorities of Jesus, when we are looking at the specific issues of our day and asking, "What would Jesus do?" the test for our actions comes from Jesus' own lips: Love God and love your neighbor as yourself. What I find really interesting is that when Jesus ties together those two commands, he gives the first and then says the second is "like it." The original Greek word there is *homoios* and it means "similar." By putting those two things together and saying the second is like the first, Jesus is telling us that loving our neighbors as ourselves is the way that we express our love of God. Love of God *is* love of neighbor.

So there's no room for me to claim that I'm stomping on you out of my unwavering devotion to God and God's laws. From Jesus himself we hear that the greatest command is that we show our love for God by lifting up our neighbors, by tending to their wounds and seeing to their needs, as the Good Samaritan did for the wounded man he found on the road. If we follow Jesus' actions through the Gospels, we find that most of the time he is doing just that.

And then in Matthew 25:31–46 we see that, while love of neighbor might be hard, it isn't rocket science. It looks like everything you would expect: Feeding the hungry, welcoming strangers, giving water to the thirsty and clothing to the naked, visiting those sick and in prison. Love, as it turns out, is not mustering some warm fuzzy feeling for someone. Love is a behavior. It's an action verb that simply asks us to extend a hand to those who have fallen, because it will take all of us to get to that promised land of peace and justice. Nobody is to be left in a ditch. Either we all go, or nobody goes. In that sense, when we help out someone else, we are also helping ourselves.

So, lo and behold, love of neighbor is not only the same as love of God, it's also the same as love of self. The genius of the Great Commandment is that it's actually all one thing said in three different ways. We express our love of God by loving our neighbors, which is the way that we ourselves inherit eternal life.

The genius of the Great Commandment is that it's actually all one thing said in three different ways. We express our love of God by loving our neighbors, which is the way that we ourselves inherit eternal life.

So, when we consider our position on a given issue or when we ponder how we should go about working for what we believe in, our decisions have to pass the test of the Great Commandment for us to say that our priorities are in line with God's. Is it loving in a way that lifts all boats? Then, go ahead. Or as St. Augustine of Hippo famously said, "Love God, and do what you will."[1]

Priority Three: Don't Make It About You

What I would list as God's third priority is a word from the prophet Micah that gives helpful definition to the other two. While it doesn't have quite the weight of tradition that either the Great Commandment or the Ten Commandments holds, it's hard to find a better summary of God's priorities than Micah 6:8: "He has told you, O mortal, what is good; and what does the LORD require of you, but to do justice, and to love kindness, and to walk humbly with your God?"

While the Great Commandment tells us that love of God, neighbor, and self should be the motivation for all we do and the Ten Commandments warn us about specific pitfalls that could throw that project off-course, Micah tells us that our attitude as we go about it all is key. He lays it out in three parts.

1. **Do justice**. The goal for which we work is justice. Don't just talk about justice; don't just read books about justice. Do something. Actively work to

---

[1] From *In epistulam Ioannis ad Parthos* (*Tractatus* VII, 8). In context, the passage reads, "Once for all, then, a short precept is given unto you: Love God, and do what you will: whether you hold your peace, through love hold your peace; whether you cry out, through love cry out; whether you correct, through love correct; whether you spare, through love do you spare: In all things, let the root of love be within, for of this root can nothing spring but what is good." From *Nicene and Post-Nicene Fathers*, First Series, vol. 7, H. Browne, trans., Philip Schaff, ed. (Buffalo, NY: Christian Literature Publishing Co., 1888). Revised and edited for New Advent by Kevin Knight, http://www.newadvent.org/fathers/170207.htm.

make sure everyone is treated fairly and equally, especially by the law of the land. The Hebrew word here is *mishpat*, which has a legal sense, so in the first phrase Micah asks us to be sure not only that laws are enforced, but that the laws themselves are just. Enforcing an unjust law makes things worse, not better. There are many ways to engage that work, but it takes all of us, using our own unique gifts and opportunities, to get the whole project over the finish line. God expects every one of us, in our own way, to do justice.

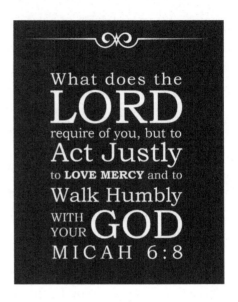

2. **Love mercy**. When enforcing the law—whether in your nation, workplace, or home—show mercy. See every person as a human being, made in the image of God. Be a channel for God's kindness, even when someone has transgressed the rules in some way. Jesus reminds us that being merciful in judgment perfectly balances love of neighbor and love of self, "for with the judgment you make you will be judged, and the measure you give will be the measure you get." (Matthew 7:2) Or, if you like the Lord's Prayer better, "forgive us our debts, as we forgive our debtors." (Matthew 6:12) Our own approach to those who break the law gives God a roadmap for what to do when we run afoul of the law ourselves. Do you want mercy for your own transgressions? Extend it to others. Seems fair.

3. **Walk humbly**. In walking through this life with God, be humble about it. God chose each of us for service to the world, not for privileges for ourselves. It's not about us; it's about loving God with all we have. Or, as Jesus would later say it in Matthew 6:1, "beware of practicing your piety before others in order to be seen by them; for then you have no reward from your Father in heaven." It's critical to recognize our own unique gifts. Whatever we're really good at is a clue to figuring out what God is calling us to do. Being humble is not pretending we're too inept to tie our own shoes, when we're in fact the

person who invented shoelaces. It's being honest about the source of our gifts and talents and recognizing that we have them in order to serve the world.

The Great Commandment, the Ten Commandments, and Micah 6:8 have my vote as a summary of God's priorities. Whatever other laws and injunctions we might find in the Bible, I believe they are to be interpreted in light of those three things. Those are the core principles that, if followed by enough people, would result in a promised land of justice, peace, and abundance for all. Maybe there are other passages of Scripture or other core values you would include. If you're doing this as a group, you'll have a chance to share those with one another as you talk about what justice means to you in light of the issues we face.

VISIONS OF JUSTICE

Living by those values is critically important, but it's also hard. To help keep us on track, we have symbolic reminders of our ideals. When it comes to justice, most of us living in the West are familiar with the images of Lady Justice with her blindfold, sword, and scales. The blindfold represents the belief that justice should be impartial. The sword she holds represents the authority to enforce justice, and the scales stand for the need to weigh evidence and balance competing claims. Some depictions of Lady Justice show her with a snake under her foot, indicating the power of justice over corruption. She is often pictured supported by books—sometimes the body of laws for a nation, sometimes a sacred text like the Bible—showing that justice is supported by law and/or the faithful interpretation of a religious text. Sometimes there is a lamp to symbolize knowledge.

At the United States Supreme Court those common symbols of justice have been divided into two statues of seated figures, which sit on either side of the main steps. On one side is a statue called "Contemplation of Justice." It's a woman holding a smaller Lady Justice statue in her lap. Her left arm rests on a large book of laws. The statue she holds has the familiar scales and blindfold. On the opposite side of the steps is a male figure. This statue is called "Authority of Law" and he holds a sheathed sword and a book of laws, held up for all to see.[2]

---

2   Carved by James Earle Fraser; installed in November 1935.

Statue of Lady Justice on the Well of Justice in Bern, Switzerland

Because those symbols are usually found in courthouses and law offices, we tend to think of justice and law as being the same thing, but they're not. Law is supposed to be the process by which the outcome of justice is achieved. It falls short way too often and this entire series will look at the reasons for that, but the theory is sound. The symbols of the blindfold, scales, sword, and so on are reminders that if we create and enforce our laws with those principles in mind, justice will result. And that's great. They are inspirational symbols for lawmakers and judges.

Supreme Court of the United States

What those symbols don't do, however, is provide much motivation for us as citizens to do the hard work of following the law. We might find a bit of urgency in looking at the sword, but how many of you have seen a statue of Lady Justice and come away vowing to be a better human being? Judges may see the blindfold and appreciate the reminder to be impartial. But how many felons look at a statue of Lady Justice and come away totally reformed?

Just like children are rarely satisfied with following orders simply "because I said so," most of us would like an inspirational reason to obey the law. We understand the whole "if you don't, you're going to jail" thing. But do we really want to live in a society where people keep the law only because they're too scared not to? In the U.S. at least, we don't really have a shared, inspirational vision of the world we could have if "liberty and justice for all" became a reality. It's a sad state of affairs that we usually get such inspiring images only from Coke and Hallmark commercials. For those willing to open it up, however, the Bible can provide the inspiration we seek.

The biblical laws have the same relationship to justice as our own laws do. They are meant as a guide for human behavior that, if followed with wisdom and good faith, would result in justice for the people. To be sure, the Bible has its share of threats for those who break the law. And, just as in every modern nation, many of those laws change with the times and circumstances. But those threats and shifts are more than balanced by the timeless, inspirational images of what the world could be if everyone got it right. Instead of providing symbols only for lawmakers and judges, the Bible inspires the people directly.

The overriding theme of the Bible is not threat, but promise. "Do this, and you will live." Through Holy Days, Sabbaths, and festivals, the community remembers their liberation and celebrates not just what was and what is, but what could be. The prophets balance their warnings of dire outcomes with the promises of streams in the desert and a time when mourning is turned to dancing. And both testaments give us visions of an age when justice and peace are ensured: A time when predator and prey lie down together in peace with a little child to lead them (Isaiah 11); a day when all nations will stream through heaven's gates for healing; when death, tears, and pain will be no more (Revelation 21).

While all the laws from long ago seem arcane, confusing, and more violent than we think warranted, the lives of the biblical characters show us clearly the attitudes and behaviors that lead either toward or away from those heavenly visions. In Jesus, the New Testament gives a living, breathing example of the kind of life that leads to those heavenly visions becoming reality. From Jesus, we learn that to "do justice," as Micah directed, doesn't mean merely to live a law-abiding life. It means a life that considers others and not just ourselves, a life where leading means serving and where the first go last, not as a punishment but because they delight in lifting people up and can't imagine having something themselves while others go without. Jesus is love incarnate, and when love meets law, you have justice. When love reigns in the kingdom of God, justice for all is a given because love of God, neighbor, and self are all the same thing.

... when love meets law, you have justice.

ALL JUSTICE IS SOCIAL

Justice in the Bible isn't an abstract concept. There is no "believing" in justice as an intellectual exercise separate from actively working to bring it about. We have to get out there with other people and do our part. For those who have taken God's name by saying yes to God's offer of relationship, justice involves participation in actions that positively affect others.

As we do so, we need to be sure we're looking at the whole picture. In many quarters there are distinctions made between "acts of charity" and "acts of justice." A number of churches today embrace acts of charity but intentionally stay away from "justice ministries," believing them to belong to the political and legal realms of society rather than to the church. The Bible makes no such distinction. In the Bible, justice is the outcome of living out God's priorities day to day. Our view of what constitutes a charitable act is often too limited.

The best illustration I know for this is the following parable about a town by a river:

> Once upon a time, there was a town that was built just beyond the bend of a large river. One day some of the children from the town were playing beside the river when they noticed three bodies floating in the water. They ran for help and the townsfolk quickly pulled the bodies out of the river.
>
> One body was dead so they buried it. One was alive, but quite ill, so they put that person into the hospital. The third turned out to be a healthy child, who then they placed with a family who cared for it and who took it to school.
>
> From that day on, every day a number of bodies came floating down the river and, every day, the good people of the town would pull them out and tend to them—taking the sick to hospitals, placing the children with families, and burying those who were dead.
>
> This went on for years; each day brought its quota of bodies, and the townsfolk not only came to expect a number of bodies each day but also worked at developing more elaborate systems for picking them out of the

river and tending to them. Some of the townsfolk became quite generous in tending to these bodies and a few extraordinary ones even gave up their jobs so that they could tend to this concern full-time. And the town itself felt a certain healthy pride in its generosity.

However, during all these years and despite all that generosity and effort, nobody thought to go up the river, beyond the bend that hid from their sight what was above them, and find out why, daily, those bodies came floating down the river.[3]

Too frequently our "acts of charity" are defined only as caring for the bodies that come down the river. We see someone suffering and we help. That's absolutely necessary. The only time Jesus gives us any specifics about how we will be judged is in how we respond in exactly those situations: Feed the hungry, clothe the naked, welcome the stranger, etc. (Matthew 25:31–46)

But in a large society and an interconnected world, that response alone is playing whack-a-mole. When the bodies turn up day after day after day, charity also requires someone to step up and ask, "Why? What is going on upriver that is causing this constant flow of bodies? And how can we go beyond meeting their daily needs and fix the system that's responsible for this mess?" Work related to that second question is typically defined as "acts of justice," but making a distinction between that work and the work of directly meeting the needs of individuals can create a whole new set of problems.

A local man helps a Syrian refugee as he swims ashore to the island of Lesbos.

Separating charity from justice is like separating a symptom from the disease. Yes, people need relief from the symptoms in the moment; but if we're not also addressing the cause of those symptoms, our charity can turn to ashes. Let's

---

3   Ronald Rolheiser, *The Holy Longing: The Search for a Christian Spirituality* (New York: Doubleday, 1999). Copyright © 1999 by Ronald Rolheiser. Used with permission of Doubleday, an imprint of the Knopf Doubleday Publishing Group, a division of Penguin Random House LLC. All rights reserved. Used with permission.

say a church helps people with vouchers for food, gas, or heat. Many churches do that, and in my view they should. But when they do, it isn't long before they start to see the same faces on a regular basis. And that's where problems can crop up. There are two questions a church seeking justice should ask at this point: "How do we care for these?" and "Why is this happening over and over?" To ask only one is to invite trouble and, eventually, spiritual decay.

The majority of churches ask only the "how" question. Some decide they can't meet the needs at all, some develop large and elaborate systems to meet them, and most fall somewhere in between. They might operate soup kitchens, food pantries, thrift shops, or have vouchers for gas, oil, and help with utility bills. But no matter the size of the response, the need is always larger. If no one is asking the "why" question, the bodies continue to flow down the river, workers and churches become overwhelmed, and the eventual response from many is resentment.

Some jump to the conclusion that the people who return for help frequently are abusing the church's generosity or somehow taking advantage. The economic toll can lead us to start making distinctions between "givers" and "takers," between people who "deserve" our care and people who don't. We fault their planning or budgeting or life's decisions because no one is looking up the river to see what's really going on. If we had someone up there investigating, they could help us understand why those approaches aren't working for those washing up on our doorstep, transforming our resentment into compassionate, long-term solutions.

On the flip side, churches that only ask the "why" question also have problems. The "how" question is difficult in terms of its scale. It grows and grows and grows, until our values crumble under the weight of need. The "why" question is difficult because of its complexity. If you ask why the person at your door can't buy their own food and really try to get to the bottom of the issue, you are soon engulfed with issues of education, disability, discrimination, abuse, addiction, class, and mental illness, to name just a few. And often those things are layered over each other. Addressing those issues requires working with community groups, federal agencies, the courts, and lawmakers at all levels.

It isn't surprising that most churches avoid opening that box; it's hard and can require very specific skills. But for those who do, there's also a danger.

Dealing only with the "why" question can lead to partisanship and a disdain for those whose calling is to help with the "how" side of the equation. While making much-needed progress up the river, those who are still being harmed can be left without care, giving a church a reputation as merely a political operator with no real heart for those suffering in the moment. Charity and justice are not separate acts. Charity is a holistic approach to care that alleviates the symptoms of injustice while also finding and treating the source.

Charity and justice are not separate acts. Charity is a holistic approach to care that alleviates the symptoms of injustice while also finding and treating the source.

If we ask both the "how" and the "why" questions, we quickly come to understand that all justice is social—we can't possibly do this by ourselves. Justice is beyond the resources of any one individual or community. Paul's metaphor of the Body of Christ is instructive here.

Priority Two: The Great Commandment

For just as the body is one and has many members, and all the members of the body, though many, are one body, so it is with Christ. For in the one Spirit we were all baptized into one body—Jews or Greeks, slaves or free—and we were all made to drink of one Spirit. Indeed, the body does not consist of one member but of many. If the foot would say, "Because I am not a hand, I do not belong to the body," that would not make it any less a part of the body. And if the ear would say, "Because I am not an eye, I do not belong to the body," that would not make it any less a part of the body. If the whole body were an eye, where would the hearing be? If the whole body were hearing, where would the sense of smell be? But as it is, God arranged the members in the body, each one of them, as he chose. If all were a single member, where would the body be? As it is, there are many members, yet one body. —1 Corinthians 12:12–20

We all have our function in the body, but that doesn't mean we don't need the other limbs and organs. If one church can operate a soup kitchen, wonderful! Team up with another group running a community garden to provide the produce. And while the hungry are being fed, connect with churches or organizations who are sending out their lawyers, politicians, and advocates to convince towns to make space for those community gardens, to provide affordable and nutritious food in schools, affordable housing, and addiction recovery programs. Their success will keep your soup kitchen manageable, and your hands-on experience will give a human face to their efforts and stories of real lives that will make their work compelling to the larger forces they seek to influence. Join together to form one body with many parts, led by our highest values. When that happens, the outcome is justice—our promised land, our true home.

BELOVED COMMUNITY

PRETENDERS

How to Spot an Idol

All justice issues are, at their heart, a longing for home. For people of all faiths and no faith alike, the concept of "home" is equated with peace and belonging, even if our actual homes give us neither. In *The Wizard of Oz*, when Dorothy finally clicks her ruby slippers together and earnestly repeats, "There's no place like home," somewhere deep inside our souls we understand. It might be an experience we once had and would like to find again or it might be a place "somewhere over the rainbow," but the idea of home is a place where we can expect both justice and mercy, a place where our highest values are embodied and lived, and a place where there are absolutely, positively no flying monkeys.

Dorothy singing "Somewhere Over the Rainbow" in The Wizard of Oz (1939)

And yet we have such trouble getting there. Why? Perhaps, like Dorothy, we are too frightened by the fire and smoke of a powerful image to check behind the curtain in the back. We accept the claim that something represents God's values, but never put that claim to the test. We could go home any time we wish, but are diverted from the path time and again by the promise of a carnival barker from Kansas who claims to be the great and powerful Wizard of Oz. And then, once he has us under his spell, we're surrounded by flying monkeys, fighting for our lives, and further from home than we've ever been.

That diversion is exactly what idols do. The idol may not have a human face. Idols also can be ideas or objects, places or symbols. But they all claim to represent our highest values, tricking us into leaving the difficult path toward justice with offers of magical fixes and enhanced power. The idol then manipulates our efforts and ultimately our values to serve its own purposes and we find our problems getting worse instead of better. If we voice suspicion, the idol screams and the fires flare: "Pay no attention to that man behind the curtain!" And we think twice about going over there. But then some plucky little terrier gives the curtain a tug and the jig is up. With the idol exposed, its power shrinks to its normal size and the work of justice can again move forward. We can then rejoin the path that will take us home.

In the last chapter we looked at three places in the Bible that summarize God's priorities—those observable traits that assure us that the true God is at work: the Ten Commandments; love God and your neighbor as yourselves; and to do justice, love mercy, and walk humbly with your God. Since plucky little dogs aren't always available to pull back the curtain and expose false gods, in this chapter we'll learn how to use those priorities to test the claims of the powerful things in our lives. Do they truly represent our highest values? Is there evidence that they put those first things first? Are their actions helping to create our dream home of a just and merciful world, or are they merely pretenders, exploiting our good faith for their own ends?

NO OTHER GODS

While the Ten Commandments as a whole are one of God's priorities, the commandments also have a priority among themselves. That's why this first volume is focused on just the first few commandments. Keeping the earliest ones makes keeping the rest of them easier. It's like buttoning a shirt. If you don't get the first button right, someone will post your picture on social media and people across the world will be laughing at you in minutes. If you get it wrong at the outset, nothing that follows works as intended. The commandments that start the list of the Ten are like that first button, and those first few commands in Exodus 20:1–7 can be summed up this way: The God who freed you comes first, so don't go making other things into gods or you will have called yourselves God's people in vain.

If you're Roman Catholic or Lutheran that's two commandments, and if you're from other Christian traditions it's three, and I've included a chart so you can see how different groups count them. But our concern here is that those seven verses in Exodus emphasize that becoming part of God's people means making God's priorities our own. Whatever else might be important and sacred and holy to us, whatever else we might revere, maintaining our relationship with the God who liberated us comes first.

Commandment	Jewish (Talmudic)	Anglican, Reformed, and other Christian	Orthodox	Catholic, Lutheran
I am the Lord your God	1	preface	1	1
You shall have no other gods before me	2	1		
You shall not make for yourself an idol		2	2	
You shall not make wrongful use of the name of your God	3	3	3	2
Remember the Sabbath and keep it holy	4	4	4	3
Honor your father and mother	5	5	5	4
You shall not murder	6	6	6	5
You shall not commit adultery	7	7	7	6
You shall not steal	8	8	8	7
You shall not bear false witness against your neighbor	9	9	9	8
You shall not covet your neighbor's wife	10	10	10	9
You shall not covet anything that belongs to your neighbor				10

So in everything we say and do, we need to consider God's values as we outlined them in the last chapter. If we accept that covenant, which Christians typically do at baptism, we have taken God's name for ourselves. If we elevate something else to God's place—if a different set of values becomes more important—our vows are meaningless. We have taken God's name in vain. If we get those first priorities right, all the more specific commandments that follow are natural outcomes. If these top values are ousted, however, all bets are off with keeping the rest of them.

It's not easy. The first button on that shirt is a doozy. Whether you see them as God's values or simply identify a set of human virtues that you believe are critical for living life with integrity, such a moral code is not easy to live by or even easy to identify in many of the situations in which we find ourselves. So this first volume is going to help us gain a more nuanced understanding of these first commands, especially the nature and function of idols in today's world.

The notion of idols, or "graven images," as the King James version of the Bible calls them, can be easy to misinterpret, sometimes with sad or tragic consequences. My heart broke for a man who recently emailed me to ask if displaying photographs of his deceased loved ones was breaking the commandment against making images. (It isn't.) For a more destructive example, take a tour of the old cathedrals of Britain. It's hard to find one whose statuary and bas reliefs have not been vandalized by Protestants who thought they were a violation of the command not to make graven images. Shown here is a decapitated figure from the Lady

Defaced statue at Ely Cathedral in Cambridgeshire, England

Chapel in England's Ely Cathedral. The head of almost every human carved there has been cut off, not by those who hate religion but by those whose religious zeal led them to believe the carved images violated the commandment against idols. I don't believe such severe interpretations serve us well, despite the fact that I'm a Protestant of Scottish descent and at least some of my ancestors probably participated in all that.

Iconoclast

According to Merriam-Webster, an iconoclast is: "1: a person who attacks settled beliefs or institutions 2: a person who destroys religious images or opposes their veneration." They explain that it comes from the word icon. "An icon is a picture that represents something. The most common icons today are those little images on our computers and smartphones that represent a program or function, but in the still-recent past, the most common icons were religious images. . . . Iconoclast literally means 'image destroyer.'"

Ancient Indus Valley Terracotta Female Fertility Idol—circa 3,300–2,000 B.C.E.

The most important thing to understand is that to call something an idol is to talk about how it functions, not about what it is. If it functions as the central power in your life and it's not aligned with the priorities of God we saw in the last chapter, then it's a false god—an idol. If it's important but doesn't displace God's values, it's fine.

Here's an example: Imagine that an archaeologist dug up a statue of an ancient fertility goddess and put it on a shelf in her house. That carving may well have functioned as an object of worship for whoever first owned it. But if our archaeologist keeps it as a reminder to keep on digging and to share her knowledge about ancient cultures, the image on her shelf isn't an idol. It's an object that once functioned as an idol for someone else, but for our archaeologist, it's merely a stone carving with no divine power.

She probably values that statue very much, but she doesn't consult it in the morning for advice on her day. She doesn't bring it gifts, or sing hymns praising its glory and power. She would feel a great sense of loss if it were stolen or destroyed, but she wouldn't violate her most important values to keep it. For her, it doesn't function as a god and therefore is not an idol, even if that exact same object once launched a war to protect its perceived power and authority over a city.

To prove my point that an idol describes a function rather than an object, come with me back to the Israelites in the desert and an odd story from Numbers 21.

In this story the people are pretty done with the whole desert experience. They're tired and cranky. God's miracle may have fed them manna from heaven, but even miracle food gets old when the menu never changes. So they complain. Loudly. God thinks they should have a better attitude and sends them poisonous snakes. Now they really have something to complain about, and they run to Moses to demand that he ask God to take the snakes away.

Here's where it gets interesting. God doesn't remove the snakes. Instead, God tells Moses, "Make a poisonous serpent, and set it on a pole; and everyone who is bitten shall look at it and live." So the God who just gave them a commandment not to make graven images tells Moses to make a graven

image. Moses follows orders, and it works. Whoever got bitten by a snake could run to the serpent on the pole, look at it, and live.

What happens over time is perfectly predictable. Pretty soon that snake on a pole has a name. They call it "Nehushtan," and they take it with them to the Promised Land. Soon the people are crediting the healing power to the carved snake rather than to the God who worked through it. Hundreds of years later the new King in Israel, Hezekiah, destroys Nehushtan because it has ceased to function as a vehicle for God's healing and, for too many people, has taken God's place. It has become an idol. (2 Kings 18:4)

That story shows us that images have their place. God was the one who told Moses to make the snake in the first place. The problem wasn't having an important, holy object that people relied on for healing. The problem was confusing a powerful object with the God who was the source of that power. If any given object, creature, activity, or person is recognized as an agent of God's blessing, it's good. You can love it; you can use it if it helps you; you can even set it apart for special, ritual use. That's what the word "holy" in Hebrew actually means—"set apart." We can have holy things, admire holy people, and be moved to greater devotion by sacred art. But if any of those same things come to be worshipped in themselves—apart from the God who works through them—then the good, helpful, and holy thing becomes an idol that draws people away from God and God's priorities.

EVERYTHING IN ITS PLACE

If we think of idols as only religious objects, however, we will have missed the more insidious idols in both our culture and the Bible. Consider the New Testament story of the Rich Young Ruler in Mark 10. A rich young man comes to see Jesus and asks what he needs to do to inherit eternal life. Jesus tells him simply to keep the commandments, referring to the Ten. The young man responds with the amazing claim that he's done just that since his youth. Been there, done that; I've kept them all, the man says. Jesus, with incredible insight, puts that claim to the test.

He starts with the very first commandment, to see if there is anything that this young man has put above the God of Israel. "You lack one thing," says Jesus. "Go and sell all that you have and give to the poor. Then come and follow me." *Ouch!* Jesus has just stepped on the young man's god. The man considers the request, hangs his head, and walks away sad. He can't do it. Not only is he unable to do what Jesus asks, he realizes that he has *not* kept all the commandments since his youth. He hasn't even kept the first one. He has put his material possessions before God. His wealth has become an idol.

This story is not a condemnation of wealth or a command for everyone to give up all their possessions. If it were, that would have been Jesus' first answer to the young man's question. But it wasn't. Jesus first answered the man's question by telling him to follow the commandments. It was only after the man said he was doing so already that Jesus tested the claim by asking him to give up the thing Jesus guessed would be hardest—the thing that functions as an idol both then and now perhaps more than any other—wealth.

Just a few verses down from the story of the rich young man, Peter tells Jesus, "Look, we have left everything and followed you." (Mark 10:28) Exactly. If the Rich Young Ruler hadn't made an idol out of his wealth, subsequent history might have spoken of Jesus' thirteen disciples instead of just the twelve. "Leave it all and follow me" was exactly the call that got the others on board. The start of discipleship for them as well as for us is the test of the first commandment: Is there something we refuse to give up in order to find our true home? If a just world lies in one direction, is there anything that can compel us to turn the other way instead? Those answers reveal our true priorities.

Christ and the Rich Young Ruler by Heinrich Hofmann, 1889

This story shows us again that the idolatry commandment is about function, not the thing itself. When Peter points out that he and the other disciples have all given up everything, Jesus doesn't pat him on the back and say, "Good! In God's kingdom, nobody is allowed to have anything." Instead, Jesus assures him that those who have given up everything will get it all back a hundredfold both now and in the age to come. In other words, by giving them up to follow Jesus, the disciples proved that everything they left behind was in its proper place in their lives. Their priorities were in order. Because they proved capable of keeping the main thing the main thing, they could have all they gave up back, with interest.

God's people are allowed to have material things, deep relationships, important allegiances, and a host of values. But they are not allowed to let those things take priority over the command to love God and our neighbors as ourselves. They must not interfere with us reflecting God's love in the world through humble service. They must not block us from doing justice and caring for "the least of these." If they do, they have become an idol that must be put back in its place if we want any semblance of justice here on this side of the rainbow. The biblical vision of "home" is not austere and sterile. It's a place where the fruits of love are evident everywhere, a welcoming place of joyful abundance, justice, and peace. Everything that serves those ends is allowed, in its place. That place just can't be first or the whole project is at risk.

Okay, but aren't we here to talk about social issues? How do all these dots of home and justice, idols and priorities connect? Here's my underlying assumption for this entire series: When a lesser set of priorities muscles its way to the top (i.e., becomes an idol), our efforts to solve our very real problems become stalled or diverted. Why? Because it's only God's ultimate priorities that can lead us to that home of peace and justice. To really achieve "liberty and justice for all," lesser values have to be moved out of the seats of power and into a supporting role.

It's not that those other things aren't good. It's just that other values simply are not suited to ultimate power, and ultimate power is needed to achieve our greatest goals. If anything less is allowed to run the show, get ready for flying monkeys. Division and anger will follow as justice is thwarted, and in very short order a social *problem* becomes an intractable social *issue*.

Those wielding that lesser power can acknowledge and correct the error, in which case the path to justice can be followed again. More commonly, however, the lesser power refuses to give up the more powerful seat and corrupts those who occupy it. When that happens, a web of lies and deception become necessary to stay in power by pretending that these different priorities can lead to a goal they have no chance of reaching. The carnival barker from Kansas gets a loud microphone and some pyrotechnics and hides behind a curtain to keep his power over Oz.

How does this play out in real life? Let's take a brief look at an issue that once was very divisive in the U.S. and now is manageable without rancor: Smoking cigarettes.

UP IN SMOKE

The first studies linking smoking to lung cancer were released in the 1940s and 1950s. The surgeon general and the U.S. Department of Health, Education,

and Welfare (now Health and Human Services) issued multiple reports warning of the dangers in the 1960s. As a result, health warnings first appeared on cigarette packs in 1966, and the Federal Communications Commission banned cigarette advertising on radio and television in 1971. But, just as solutions were being developed and deployed, progress came to a halt for almost thirty years. What happened? The idol of corporate profit began to feel its power eroding, and the tobacco industry mobilized to defend it.

Lobbyists for the tobacco industry reminded members of Congress that winning elections would take their support—which the industry would withhold or give according to congressional votes on smoking measures. Presidents were reminded that the road to the White House ran through tobacco states like North Carolina, Kentucky, and Tennessee.

The message registered. In administrations controlled by both Republicans and Democrats, government oversight of the industry was quietly defunded, those raising alarms were pushed out of government positions, and trade negotiations paved the way for increased tobacco sales abroad. The Food and Drug Administration decided that cigarettes were beyond its scope.[4] Progress on solving the smoking problem came to a halt.

---

4   For a detailed look at the politics of the tobacco fight see: Bente Tangvik, "President Clinton and the American Tobacco Industry" (doctoral thesis, University of Oslo, 2007), https://www.duo.uio.no/bitstream/handle/10852/25499/tangvik.pdf.

That upset anti-smoking advocates, who organized boycotts and raised their voices at the state level and with local retailers. While not part of any formal organization, my mother was a formidable foe when it came to ridding public places of cigarette smoke. The manager at our local McDonald's hated to see her coming. Every time we went in, she asked for him and complained that there was exactly one booth set aside as a non-smoking booth. "Don't you realize that any booth I sit in is automatically a non-smoking booth?" she would say. "Having just one booth does nothing at all when people are smoking all around me. The smoke doesn't know that it shouldn't enter my booth." Her father was a chain smoker, but when he visited our Rhode Island home, she sent him outside to smoke—even in sub-zero temperatures. People like my mother were raising a ruckus everywhere, while the tobacco industry continued to block federal progress.

Smokers were upset, too. They believed the tobacco industry lie that anti-smoking activism would lead to cigarettes being banned; they felt betrayed as the habit some had taken up to fit in with the "cool" crowd now diminished their standing in society instead. They bristled, too, at being bossed around: Weren't they free to decide whether or not to smoke? With the science being distorted or suppressed by the industry, smokers questioned the claims that tobacco was as bad as everyone was insisting it was. Smoking changed from a problem to be solved to a divisive social issue. Flying monkeys were everywhere.

It wasn't until the 1990s—thirty years after health warnings had been put on cigarette packs and fifty years after the first studies linking smoking to lung cancer were published—that the ground began to shift. In 1994 an anonymous tipster sent thousands of pages of documents from the Brown & Williamson tobacco company to an anti-smoking advocate at the University of California in San Francisco. Led by ABC News, media reports began to show that companies were manipulating nicotine levels in cigarettes to keep consumers hooked. Slowly the rage of many smokers turned away from those they thought were trying to take their cigarettes toward those who had tricked them into an addiction that could cost them their lives.

With the curtain pulled back, the CEOs of the seven largest U.S. tobacco companies were hauled before Congress.

Tobacco industry leaders sworn in before Congress, 1994

A particularly revealing moment in the 1994 hearing is described this way in the *New York Times*: "Mr. Wyden presented a stack of data from medical groups and a 1989 surgeon general's report on the perils of smoking, asking each executive in turn if he believed that cigarettes were addictive. Each answered no." When presented with estimates of death from smoking, one executive replied that such estimates were "generated by computers and are only statistical." The executives complained that Congress wanted to ban cigarettes entirely and warned of the black market such action would create. (They admitted, however, that they preferred their own children not smoke.[5]) Attempts to regulate the tobacco industry cost many members of Congress their seats in the 1994 midterms, as members began to refuse the bribes that once kept the idol in power.

In 1996 the issue of selling cigarettes to children finally pushed the FDA to get involved and threaten regulation. In 1998 five U.S. tobacco companies settled a lawsuit brought by forty-six states by agreeing to restrict advertising, pay more than $206 billion over twenty-five years to cover smoking-related health care costs, and to fund a national anti-smoking education foundation.

---

5   Philip J. Hilts, "Tobacco Chiefs Say Cigarettes Aren't Addictive," *New York Times*, April 15, 1994, https://www.nytimes.com/1994/04/15/us/tobacco-chiefs-say-cigarettes-aren-t-addictive.html.

But the settlement allowed them to escape regulation. After all, they argued, to pay the billions they'd been charged, they had to keep up sales. They were still in the driver's seat, but their grip on the wheel was weakening. By March 22, 2003, Philip Morris was staring down the wrong end of a different lawsuit for deceptive marketing and was hit with a $10.1 billion fine.

On August 17, 2006, U.S. District Judge Gladys Kessler found Philip Morris and its parent company, Altria Group, guilty of racketeering. Her 1,683-page opinion lambasted both the industry and its lawyers:

> [This case] is about an industry, and in particular these Defendants, that survives, and profits, from selling a highly addictive product which causes diseases that lead to a staggering number of deaths per year, an immeasurable amount of human suffering and economic loss, and a profound burden on our national health care system. Defendants have known many of these facts for at least 50 years or more. Despite that knowledge, they have consistently, repeatedly, and with enormous skill and sophistication, denied these facts to the public, to the Government, and to the public health community. . . [The lawyers] directed scientists as to what research they should and should not undertake; they vetted scientific research papers and reports as well as public relations materials to ensure that the interests of the Enterprise would be protected; they identified "friendly" scientific witnesses, subsidized them with grants. . . , paid them enormous fees, they devised and carried out document destruction policies.[6]

The initial issue of cigarettes and their health impacts was complicated and required a large coalition of forces to solve. Especially given the length of time health studies can take, the time needed to resolve this problem under normal circumstances would be a couple of decades. But that timeframe was interrupted by the same idol that derailed the discipleship of the Rich Young Ruler: money. As a result, what should have been resolved in twenty-five years took more than fifty. And while smoking is no longer a divisive issue in the U.S., the idol worshipped by the tobacco industry is still in control. The difference now is that the curtain has been pulled back. Now that we know the

---

6   United States v. Philip Morris USA Inc., et al., Civil Action No. 99-CV-2496 (2017), https://publichealthlawcenter.org/sites/default/files/resources/doj-final-opinion.pdf, 3–4.

actual priorities of the industry, the rest of us can make our decisions related to smoking based on the truth and our own highest values.

BREAKING BAD

While we will be dealing with specific social issues related to money in later volumes, the idol of the Almighty Dollar is working behind the scenes in almost every issue that divides our country today. Words generally attributed to African-American psychologist Dr. Amos N. Wilson wisely point out, "If you want to understand any problem in America, you need to focus on who profits from that problem, not who suffers from that problem."

> "If you want to understand any problem in America, you need to focus on who profits from that problem, not who suffers from that problem."
>
> AMOS N. WILSON

The idol of money is as old as money itself, and Jesus warns of it when he tells his followers in the Sermon on the Mount, "You cannot serve both God and money." (Matthew 6:24, NIV) As we know, however, money is not the only way to "profit" from a situation.

In the smoking controversy, money was the idol running the tobacco industry, but many lawmakers had an idol of their own: They literally sacrificed the lives of their constituents to keep their political power and influence. Instead of solving the smoking problem, they slow-walked the conversation and watered down any progress. In return they got funding from the industry to run their campaigns and keep their seats. In their case the money was the means, but the end—the profit that became their ultimate value—was power. And once that idol was up and running, it operated in the way all idols do. With the idol of power running the legislature and the idol of money running the tobacco industry, together they spread and maintained their influence through lies, deception, suppression of facts, and fear-mongering, frightening people into thinking a basic freedom (in this case, the freedom to choose to smoke) would be taken from them if the tobacco industry were to be regulated. We will see these tactics again and again in issue after issue.

Before going further, it needs to be said again that while idols cause serious harm, the things that become idols are not, in and of themselves, bad things. The danger of idolatry isn't a tendency to put bad things before God. The danger is taking good things and treating them like the most important things, thus opening them up to corruption. Remember: Idolatry is about how something functions, not about its fundamental nature. In the tobacco case, companies were not wrong for wanting to make a profit. That's how you stay in business. Money by itself is not a bad thing and is not an idol. It's only when money functioned as a god—when it became more important to the companies than human life and health—that things got ugly. Scripture reminds us that it is not money by itself, but the "love of money" that is the root of all evil. (1 Timothy 6:10)

It's the same thing with the desire for power and influence—a totally legitimate human aspiration. There are hundreds of self-help books about "empowerment," and public service is all about finding people with gifts that can benefit society and then giving them the power and influence to do so. Power, in and of itself, is a great good. To take all of a person's power is to enslave. Having power is freedom; things that strip us of power are generally considered human rights abuses and, in most law codes, crimes. So we have to be careful not to jump on our high horse and declare that anyone seeking power for themselves is committing idolatry.

If you work in government to make a difference in the lives of your constituents and are doing so to the best of your ability, it's not wrong to want to be reelected and continue that work. Wanting power and influence is not idolatry. It's only when the desire for power and influence becomes more important than the goal of serving the public that it becomes an idol.

That's why idols are so tricky. The most dangerous idols are all wonderful and necessary things that we have allowed to edge out the things that should be most important. The problem isn't the thing, it's the way that thing has grabbed power to which is was not entitled, power that can guide secondary values well but is unable to pilot our ultimate values to safe harbor. Because most idols are good things that are simply out of place, it can be hard to tell the true from the false, and the more powerful the idol, the harder it is. But it can be done if we stay alert and watch for the signs.

IDOLSPOTTING

Pay no attention to the man behind the curtain – Toto pulls back the curtain.

So, let's start. How do we spot an idol? There are five key signs:

- Idols bear bad fruit.
- Idols have more power than they should.
- Idols present resolutions as a zero-sum game.
- Idols spew lies and deception.
- Idols offer only binary choices.

Let's look at these signs in more detail:

Idols bear bad fruit.

In Matthew 7:15–16 Jesus says, "Beware of false prophets, who come to you in sheep's clothing but inwardly are ravenous wolves. You will know them by their fruits." The most obvious sign that we are being deceived is the presence of bad fruit.

When those in charge focus on an issue, we should expect movement toward a fair and just solution. That movement might only be continuing dialogue, but once those with the power to fix a problem have said they're on it, the process should keep going and keep improving. We should see more unity, not less. Anxiety should be decreasing, even if only a little. Fewer people should feel harmed or threatened, even if there's some trial and error along the way. Dialogue (rather than shouting) should increase. That's what good fruit looks like: There's progress, and while sides may disagree on how to get there, they agree on a common goal and continue to work together in good faith toward a win-win solution.

But if an idol is given a seat at the negotiating table, that normal movement is disrupted. We saw that in the smoking controversies we looked at earlier. Philip Morris and others knew the public would be outraged if they learned that the company was unconcerned with thousands of deaths per year as long as they made a profit. That profit was their idol, and they disguised it by hiding the evidence, paying for fake science reports, pitting smokers against non-smokers, deploying misleading advertising, buying off politicians, and more. Bad fruit, all of it.

"Pay no attention to that man behind the curtain!" they cried, in their most fearsome voice. But whistleblowers played Toto to their Oz and took the curtain in their teeth, exposing what was really happening. The U.S. court system took it from there. The idol was exposed, and our journey toward justice for smokers and non-smokers alike could continue.

That example of bad fruit shows how breaking the first commandment can endanger all the commandments that follow. At the very least, the tobacco industry broke the commandments against killing, stealing, and bearing false witness, all because they let profit have ultimate power. Profit is extremely important for a company—that's not wrong—but when placed above the values we associated with the true God in chapter one, it functions as an idol, breaking our relationships with God and with each other and thereby blocking the path toward justice.

Engaging issues is always hard work. But there's a difference between work that is hard and work that is toxic. When even getting close to an issue brings out the worst in people instead of their best; when widespread demands for justice are met with inaction; when we are told to fear or despise solutions that show compassion to all sides, something is not as it seems. Pull back the curtain. There's likely an idol in there. Bad fruit is the first and most obvious sign.

Idols have more power than they should.

Every social justice issue has, at its core, the claim of a power imbalance. The balance of power goes out of whack all the time, and the expectation of justice is that when the issue is raised, those with the power to fix it will work to bring it into balance again. But if they don't—if the power imbalance continues to exist over time with obvious signs of the problem being ignored or even encouraged—there's something more going on. The tolerance of a power imbalance by those with the power to fix it is a sure sign of the presence of an idol.

Power is the lifeblood of an idol. The things that become idols most easily are all various means of achieving power—money, celebrity, military power and weapons, political influence, religious objects or doctrines, majority status—you name it. Whatever increases our power is idol-prone, and care and attention is needed to keep it where it belongs. So, the question to ask is, "Does this thing, person, or idea at the center of the debate have more influence than it should on this issue?"

In the United States, that question is central to determining cases about the First Amendment. The rights it protects—religion, speech, the press, the voice of the people rising in peaceful protest—are all extremely powerful things. The question is not whether those things should have power. The First Amendment is designed to ensure that their power is not only established, but protected. The question is whether the power of one of those things has moved out of its lane to exercise too much power someplace else.

Chapter five will look at the First Amendment questions specifically, and other chapters will encourage you to think about that question as well. But as a general sign, it's important simply to ask whether there's a powerful player at the table that doesn't belong in the particular debate you're having. If so, keep your eyes wide open. An idol may be attempting a power grab.

Idols present resolutions as a zero-sum game.

The biblical imagery for the new heaven and new earth contains a "spring of the water of life"[7] and "the river of the water of life, bright as crystal, flowing from the throne of God and of the Lamb through the middle of the street of the city."[8] Both are a constant flow from an infinite source that ensures healing and abundance for all. When God's priorities are in charge, that belief—that there is ultimately enough for everyone—leads to healthy and just resolutions to conflict. We can love our neighbors and ourselves and both of us will be the better for it. It's the miracle of the loaves and fishes—in God's economy, the correction for scarcity is sharing.

But if an idol is in charge, the outlook changes drastically. There is no win-win in idolatry. It's a zero-sum game. There's no infinite spring of water, there's just a single glass, and if I give you any, I won't have enough. In a zero-sum game, your gain has to mean my loss. More rights for you means fewer rights for me. I planned ahead and brought my own loaves and fish for lunch. It's not my responsibility if you didn't do the same.

We can tell we're dealing with a zero-sum game when we see selfishness and hoarding. Generosity is an existential threat to an idol and its followers. Those who cry for justice are merely "takers" who want to steal something you have. With idols, all the solutions require one side to win and one side to lose, often with added humiliation for the loser so they won't ever ask again. Sharing represents loss for the idol, whether it's about resources, compassion, or power. No one else gets a thing, even if the idol and its followers are a small minority of those involved.

---

7   Revelation 21:6

8   Revelation 22:1–2

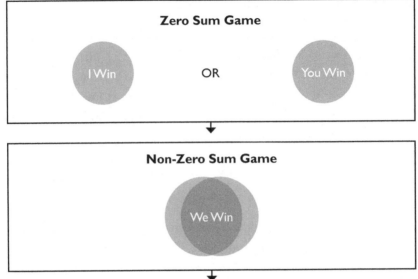

Zero Sum Game

I Win   OR   You Win

Non-Zero Sum Game

We Win

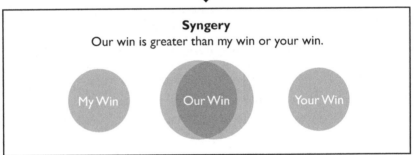

Syngery
Our win is greater than my win or your win.

My Win   Our Win   Your Win

Like with other things on this list, the presence of a zero-sum game is a sign but not a sure indicator. There are legitimate times when more over here does mean less over there. But with idols it is *always* a zero-sum game, making it easier to keep us divided from each other.

So for this test, check for generosity and a willingness to share. The more you see of that, the less likely it is that an idol is running the show. Are the proposed solutions to problems win-win or win-lose? Idols will always choose the latter. Are those in need seen as a threat to what others have? If one group asks for justice, is the response, "Well, yeah, but what about me?" If so, look around. Something's likely hiding behind the curtain.

Idols spew lies and deception.

Idols are inherently deceptive. They have to be, because they're pretending to be something they're not. That can even include claiming to be Christian or whatever other belief system is valued by those they seek to manipulate. After all, they are, in essence, claiming to be God. No one should be surprised that religious institutions and those who represent them are just as prone to idolatry as anyone else—sometimes more so. Those who want to be seen as gods try to get as close as they can to what they perceive to be the seat of God's power on earth. It's easier to slide in unnoticed when you're supposed to be in the vicinity anyway.

To justify its power, an idol claims to represent God's ultimate priorities and does everything it can to keep those who buy into that lie from discovering the truth. Every single cult works like this, whether it's a religious cult, a political cult, a gang, or a terrorist group. Cult leaders of all types look for people on the margins of society, isolate them from dissenting voices by demonizing others, and then proclaim they are the sole source of truth. Most cults go to great lengths to cut people off from their families and friends or any outside influence. They have to. The more people can sit and reason together without undue influence or threat, the more likely they are to question the status quo and wonder if there isn't a better way. Such conversations are the beginning of the end of the idol's power. For the idol to remain, its followers must be separated from other people and alternative ideas at all costs.

Whether they are the center of an actual cult or not, almost all idols pretend that they really stand for God's values as we've outlined them. They project the image that their goals are to care for all people—to love our neighbors as ourselves. Depending on the idol, this could require a lot of deception or a little. In the worst cases, entire groups of people are cast as enemies of God, resulting in violence and even genocide. But for now, consider a much milder example. Consider the humble Subaru.

Full disclosure here: I drive a Subaru and I like my car. But I can't help but cringe a bit at their slogan: "Love. It's what makes a Subaru a Subaru." Uh, no. God is love. Subaru is a brand of car. God doesn't sit at the end of the factory assembly line and infuse each Subaru with unconditional love before it rolls out to one of their "Share the Love" events.

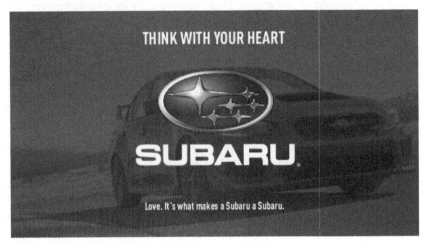

Subaru does give a portion of the sale to a charity. Great. I like that, and the charities I was given to pick from were solid. But the subconscious message of Subaru's advertising is that they share God's ultimate priority. The underlying message of their ad campaign is that buying their product doesn't just get you a good car, it makes you a better person. I can definitely drive in snow better with my Subaru. But it doesn't make me a better human. To the extent that my monthly car payments could otherwise be used to help those in need, it could be argued that my heated seats and backup camera have made me a worse person.

Watch out for the subtle deceptions that surround us daily. Sometimes the lies are blatant and dangerous and sometimes they're more nuanced and a smaller stretch of the truth. But, by definition, an idol pretends to be more powerful and important than it has a right to be. It's a false god. Deception and lies are necessary for an idol to gain and maintain power.

John 8:32 says, "You will know the truth, and the truth will make you free." The truth will set you free of idols. Ask yourself whether this person or thing is claiming to be the source of truth, the fount from which all good springs. Are you either blatantly or subtly being told to distrust all the people and sources that have helped you in the past? Are your questions treated like threats? If so, put on the brakes. This thing may not be what it seems.

Idols offer only binary choices.

Perhaps the biggest lie of any idol is that if we don't put it first, we won't have it at all. Since the things that we turn into idols are, in their proper place, good and necessary things, that all-or-nothing lie creates a fear that something we need will be taken from us if we don't keep the idol in first place. "Give an inch and they'll take a mile." Therefore the idol will not give even an eighth of an inch. If you don't let the idol have the absolute top spot, it threatens to take all its marbles and go home, leaving you with nothing. That, of course, is terrifying, which is why the tactic is used in the first place. Fear of losing that which we value is a major weapon in the idol's arsenal.

This sign is more difficult to spot than some of the others because just a casual glance around the world shows us that there are indeed forces ready to take even our most basic liberties if we're not careful, and sometimes even if we are. The fear of the slippery slope is a real one and is, therefore, easy to exploit. It almost always comes with an enemies list of those who try to put even the slightest check on the idol's power.

I've listed this sign last because it's also the tactic that keeps all the others in place. If anyone who questions the absolute authority of the idol is labeled an enemy, that keeps people isolated from different opinions, both by making others objects of fear and by making the idol's followers fearful of being labeled enemies themselves. And by keeping them isolated, no one dares to ask questions or voice suspicions about what is really going on.

Throughout the Bible, God has a give and take with the people. God's not happy that Israel wants a permanent temple in a settled location. God isn't thrilled with them having a king either. But the people get their way. God works with them. Job is allowed to challenge God's justice and still comes out blameless in God's eyes. Jesus spends a ton of time taking questions from friends and enemies alike and is patient with his disciples when they don't understand a parable or his actions. Even when the Rich Young Ruler decides he can't give up his wealth, Jesus doesn't condemn him. He just sadly lets him go. You don't find that kind of flexibility where idols rule.

You can often detect this sign in the language around an issue. My bias will show here, but I've heard people yelling, "They're trying to take your guns!" for my entire adult life, and I haven't noticed any shortage of weapons on our streets. While gun *ownership* hit a forty-year low in 2016, gun *purchases* are at an all-time high.[9] It's beginning to look more like a marketing tactic for gun manufacturers than any legitimate concern. I also haven't had any problems celebrating Christmas, despite the war on it that I keep hearing about.

You can probably think of more examples, but what they have in common is that it's all or nothing. Even the tiniest check on the idol's power is met with dire warnings that you're going to lose what you value. When all those around us are screaming it, and we have lost our trust in our institutions, it's easy to get caught up in the fear and mistakenly add our voice to protecting

---

9   Christopher Ingraham, "American Gun Ownership Drops to Lowest in Nearly 40 Years," *Washington Post*, June 29, 2016, https://www.washingtonpost.com/news/wonk/wp/2016/06/29/american-gun-ownership-is-now-at-a-30-year-low.

an idol. Not knowing where to check the truth, we just give in to the fear and hunker down with our tribe. We can do better.

Idols are false gods and no self-respecting god wants to take second place. People trying to resolve an issue will almost always have perfectly reasonable solutions that involve just a bit of a power readjustment. When no idols are around, those sensible solutions sail through and the problem is worked out. But when solutions that sound reasonable to virtually everyone else are countered with predictions that even the slightest check on its power will result in the important thing or person being taken away or destroyed, there's an idol there that needs a lesson in humility.

Ultimately, we can spot an idol because the real God uses power differently. For those of us who look to Jesus as the revelation of God's nature and will, the differences aren't hard to see. Jesus shares even his miracle-working power with his disciples. He teaches that those who want to lead should serve and that those who want to live need to be willing to die. The last must come first; the poor, hungry, and persecuted deserve blessing. Loving your neighbor includes those who belong to a shunned ethnic group who worship differently (the Samaritans). Jesus doesn't even let other people call him "good!" (Luke 18:19) Think of an issue—any issue. How is that problem not solvable by a group of people who operate with that kind of approach to power? It still may take a group of really smart people, and they'll sometimes get the answers wrong. But the problem-solving process won't be hateful or divisive or violent. It will just be hard.

If your response to that paragraph was to think that the answer to all our problems is to make everyone become a Christian, stop right there. You're right on the edge of turning the amazing good that is Christian faith into an idol. The God of Jesus Christ doesn't do that. Certainly Jesus encouraged evangelism and the making of disciples—even hoping that all nations would come to that Light. But Jesus didn't coerce anybody. Jesus didn't become an earthly king to make everyone do what he thought was best. That was exactly what Satan tempted him to do in the wilderness, and Jesus refused.

Remember the context of the Ten Commandments. Those who were bound by them were only those who willingly chose to do so. Those who became disciples of Jesus were only those who decided that they wanted to sign on.

Iesha Evans is detained by law enforcement as she protests the shooting death of Alton Sterling near the headquarters of the Baton Rouge Police Department, July 9, 2016.

The Rich Young Ruler, a man with great potential, was allowed to walk away and keep the false god he had chosen for himself. Jesus could have risen up and led his followers to overthrow the Romans and establish a theocratic state. But he gave up his own life rather than do that, much to the dismay of many. Coercion and manipulation are not the tools of God. When you see them used, look around. There's an idol nearby—maybe even one who has taken God's name in vain.

The good news is that even the most powerful and insidious idols can be dethroned and put in their proper place. And the most effective way to remove them is to begin on the altar of our own hearts. The prevalence and power of idols in our world would be greatly diminished if Christians were on their game. If there's one place I think the Ten Commandments **should** be posted for all to see, it's in the church. If we Christians kept them—even if no one else did—the world would be a much happier place.

ON THE MARCH: PREPARING FOR YOUR SECOND GROUP SESSION

To get ready for your next group session, read the following section and think about the questions at the end. They will form part of your discussion time when you meet.

An injustice happening to some of us should be an issue for all of us. But when we aren't feeling the pain directly, we often do nothing. Sometimes we actually don't realize there's a problem. Other times we're too focused on our own problems. And too often we choose to turn a blind eye or even try to claim that the group feeling harmed is making too much of their situation.

Protest is the way those who believe their concerns are being ignored get a hearing. Protest forces those in power to pay attention by saying through their actions, "No more business as usual until you pay attention and deal with this. We've had enough!" Whether it's marching on Washington, refusing to bake a cake, kneeling during the national anthem, going on strike, boycotting a company, blocking access to an abortion clinic, stopping equipment from digging a pipeline, or tearing down a monument, those actions are signs that a group of people in society believe their concerns are not being heard and addressed.

We're not talking about just one person or family having a problem. We're talking about a critical mass of people who are feeling, rightly or wrongly, that their needs and concerns are being ignored or even undermined by the laws and systems of society. They see justice and consideration given to others, but not to them. Even if what the group experiences is legal, if the laws don't seem to be applied fairly or don't result in just outcomes, societies will be disrupted in larger and larger ways until real justice is done in a way that is plain to all.

Justice

That Justice is a blind goddess
Is a thing to which we black are wise:
Her bandage hides two festering sores
That once perhaps were eyes.

LANGSTON HUGHES[10]

We don't go from being happy and content to full-bore protest mode overnight. We try to work through the system to fix a problem. It's only when the system is unresponsive, corrupt, or otherwise abusive that we take matters into our own hands to find another way to get the change we need. So it's not helpful when people say things like, "I agree that there's a problem, I just don't think protest is the right way to address it." The lack of a response when grievances are addressed through ordinary channels is what leads to a full-blown protest in the first place.

Rev. Dr. Martin Luther King Jr. tried to explain this to white clergy who, while eager to ally themselves with Dr. King's cause, were upset at the disruption his protests caused. He replied in a letter from jail, excerpted at right. You should read the entire document, which is easily found online.[11]

---

10   Langston Hughes, "Justice," *The Collected Poems of Langston Hughes*, ed. Arnold Rampersad, assoc. ed. David Roessel (New York: Random House, 1994). Copyright © 1994 by the Estate of Langston Hughes. Used with permission of Alfred A. Knopf, an imprint of the Knopf Doubleday Publishing Group, a division of Penguin Random House LLC. All rights reserved.

11   Martin Luther King Jr., "Letter from a Birmingham Jail" (August 1963), https://web.cn.edu/kwheeler/documents/Letter_Birmingham_Jail.pdf.

"You deplore the demonstrations that are presently taking place in Birmingham. But I am sorry that your statement did not express a similar concern for the conditions that brought the demonstrations into being. I am sure that each of you would want to go beyond the superficial social analyst who looks merely at effects and does not grapple with underlying causes. I would not hesitate to say that it is unfortunate that so-called demonstrations are taking place in Birmingham at this time, but I would say in more emphatic terms that it is even more unfortunate that the white power structure of this city left the Negro community with no other alternative.

"In any nonviolent campaign there are four basic steps: collection of the facts to determine whether injustices are alive, negotiation, self-purification, and direct action. We have gone through all of these steps in Birmingham. There can be no gainsaying of the fact that racial injustice engulfs this community. Birmingham is probably the most thoroughly segregated city in the United States. Its ugly record of police brutality is known in every section of this country. Its unjust treatment of Negroes in the courts is a notorious reality. There have been more unsolved bombings of Negro homes and churches in Birmingham than in any other city in this nation. These are the hard, brutal, and unbelievable facts. On the basis of them, Negro leaders sought to negotiate with the city fathers. But the political leaders consistently refused to engage in good-faith negotiation."

MARTIN LUTHER KING JR.[12]

The United States was founded when a protest against unfair taxation began with throwing tea into Boston Harbor and ended in a Revolution to gain our independence from a king who disregarded claims for justice in his colonies. No one should be surprised by protest in the United States. It's part of our DNA; it's why our founders included the right to protest in the Constitution. The First Amendment ensures "the right of the people peaceably to assemble, and to petition the government for a redress of grievances."

---

12 King, "Letter from a Birmingham Jail."

Protest functions in a healthy society the way a stabbing pain functions in a healthy body—it's a warning sign that something is amiss. People who can't feel pain are at much greater risk for serious injury. If you can't tell that your hand is on a red-hot stove, pretty soon you won't have a hand, while the person who feels pain gets away with just a burn. A society that suppresses or ignores protest thinks everything is fine—until it isn't. Because no one could feel the warning signs, the whole society collapses like a house of cards until it can be built again on a just foundation.

Every issue we look at in this series has some form of protest associated with it. That disruptive protest elevates a "problem" that we trust someone will address to an "issue" for which the only solution is disruption.

Remember that "being heard" is the first step in resolving an issue. When we listen, if there's a true injustice, we will understand it better and be more likely to find a helpful solution. We also might discover that we allowed a simple misunderstanding to escalate into something much bigger just because we didn't take the time to listen, educate, and address the anxiety of those who were seeking change.

As we imagine our perfect world of justice and peace, protest should no more be a part of *that* vision than crying or death or pain. But as we face the world as it is today, we should honor the role that protest plays. It lets us know where our society is hurting and helps us approach that hurt with compassionate curiosity instead of disdain. Protest is a sign that we don't have justice yet. Where protest exists, there is more work to be done before we can say we have arrived. The best tools for stopping protests are not water cannons, but ears.

Questions for Reflection

- Have you ever participated in a protest of any sort? A march, a boycott, a strike, refusing to do something your job required out of principle? If so, what was that experience like? What moved you to take that action? Did you think your efforts were effective?

- Has your life ever been disrupted by the protest of others? Did you understand what was being protested? Did it make you angry? Sympathetic? How did you respond?

- Do you make your voice heard through normal channels when something is happening that you don't like? Do you vote? Contact a representative? Sign petitions? What makes you decide to act? Do you jump in right away or does it take time for you to become engaged?

- Have you ever either witnessed or been part of a protest that turned violent? How did you respond? How can authorities help ensure that protests remain peaceful?

- Have you or a company or organization you are a part of ever been the object of any kind of protest? What was the response? Was the issue resolved?

- Have you ever agreed with a cause but objected to the form of a protest? What was your objection? What do you think would be more effective if the normal channels to resolving the issues are blocked?

- Finish this sentence: "It is my hope that all who protest. . ."

CHECK-IN

Write a one-sentence answer to each of the following questions. You will be asked to share these with your group but without further comment:

What is one thing that was new to me in this material?

What is one question that this week's topic(s) raises for me?

ALLEGIANCE

How Idols Confuse Our Priorities

For many people, love of country is very close to the top of their list of motivating values. Only religion and family bonds rival it, though in some cases all three values are merged, as when a family member is a military chaplain. So our national symbols frequently evoke deep emotions in us, especially in times of crisis. For many people those emotions are soaring and positive. But during times of unrest, when life feels crushing and it appears that the country is not living up to its stated ideals, our national symbols can be a point of pain, especially when the failure is not acknowledged.

To understand this feeling, think about the holidays. Such times typically are filled with joy and celebration; but when we have suffered loss or when times are hard, the joy surrounding us becomes almost a mockery, driving those who are enduring hardship into a depression equal to the joy surrounding them. Many churches have a special service around Christmas time called "Blue Christmas" to acknowledge the extra grief that the celebration brings to those who face an empty seat at the table, an inability to provide gifts, or otherwise participate in the holiday as they once did.

That's what many feel when a moment that typically would evoke pride and patriotism—like the salute of the flag or the playing of the national anthem—meets conflicted emotions about the actions of the country or a feeling of being unwelcome, betrayed, or otherwise harmed by the nation's representatives. At such times we need the equivalent of a "Blue Christmas" service—a way to say "the celebration around me is touching my point of pain."

When we want to make a statement about something, we typically use symbols; for example, we might wear a cross to show that we profess Christian faith. Those who feel harmed by the church might express their anger against its symbols by burning a Bible or desecrating a cross. It's the same with national symbols. When we feel the country is on the right track and representing our values, we fly our flags proudly and sing the anthem with gusto. But when it seems that the country is abandoning the values it's supposed to represent, we may take out our frustration on national symbols by ignoring them, vandalizing them, or protesting them in some way.

Our national symbols are some of the most powerful things in existence. They can be used to unify us and to inspire us to be all we say we are. But their very greatness and power mean that any idol worth its salt would love to co-opt one or more of them for other purposes. The more powerful a symbol is to begin with, the more likely it is to be elevated to idol status, at least by some. A symbol that unites us can be weaponized to divide us, and our national symbols are no exception. So in this chapter we'll look at how the influence of fear, war, religion, and the examples of other nations have played a role in shaping and changing our national symbols and rituals. Finally, we'll take that awareness, along with your new idol-spotting skills and understanding of protest from the last chapter, and apply it all to the NFL protests during the national anthem.

As we look at the history of our national symbols, ideals, and related controversies, please notice how both the origins and the changes to those things coincide with the concerns and stresses happening in the country at the time. That shifting history can ground us and help us keep our bearings when someone says something like, "How about if we remove the words 'under God' from the Pledge of Allegiance?" Here's a hint: It wasn't always in there.

THE FLAG AND PLEDGE OF ALLEGIANCE

Most of us have a basic knowledge of the history of the U.S. flag. Betsy Ross is usually credited with making the first official flag for the United States, but all we have for proof is the word of her grandson, who made the claim in an 1870 presentation to the Historical Society of Pennsylvania. He claimed that George Washington was sketching out six-pointed stars and that his grandmother convinced him that five-pointed stars were much easier to make. Ross and her husband ran an upholstery business and might well have made the first flag.[13] But there were other flag makers in Philadelphia. And a competing story holds that Francis Hopkinson, a member of the Continental Congress, claimed that the early flag designs were his and wrote to Congress demanding payment for them. He designed the Great Seal of the United States, so it's possible.

Apart from those ambiguous origins, the rest of our flag's history is pretty straightforward. The flag that flies over the U.S. Capitol today is the twenty-

---

13 Further exploration of this question can be found in: Laurel Thatcher Ulrich, "How Betsy Ross Became Famous: Oral Tradition, Nationalism, and the Invention of History," Common-Place (October 2007), http://www.common-place-archives.org/vol-08/no-01/ulrich.

Flag above the U.S. Capitol, Washington, DC

seventh official design. The stars and stripes that adorn it were relatively common symbols in heraldry, and there is some evidence that Benjamin Franklin wanted our flag to be a slight variant of the flag of the East India Company. (They do look very similar.) The arrangement of the stars and stripes wasn't standardized until 1912, so there were variants, especially in the shape and positioning of the stars. A few early flags even had some blue stripes.

As the nation continued to grow, the number of stars had to be constantly updated to reflect the increasing number of states. For a while, stripes as well as stars were added, but in 1818 Congress reverted to thirteen stripes to represent the thirteen original colonies. After all, flags were made of wool in those days, so even the one with thirteen stripes took eleven men to raise on a flagpole.

There is some debate about whether the flag's colors had specific meaning. The colors were given explicit meaning in the Great Seal, however, so it's natural to assume that many people would transfer that meaning to the same colors in the flag. In the Great Seal, red symbolizes hardiness and valor, white symbolizes purity and innocence, and blue represents vigilance, perseverance, and justice.

I PLEDGE ALLEGIANCE

Mrs. Claire Cumberbatch, leader of the Bedford-Stuyvesant group protesting alleged "segregated" school, leads oath of allegiance. New York, 1958.

Surprisingly, the United States of America went through 116 years of existence and 23 variations of the flag without any spoken pledge, at least not one that had wide recognition. It was a Baptist minister, Rev. Francis Bellamy, who finally provided one in 1892. But why did we suddenly get a pledge, written by a private citizen, in 1892?

When you want to understand events in the past or the present, don't just ask, "Why is this happening?" Your answer will give you much more insight if you ask, "Why is this happening *now*?" So the first thing to ask about the Pledge of Allegiance is "What was going on in the U.S. in 1892? What problem did it take a pledge to the flag to solve?"

The pledge, it turns out, was created during the Gilded Age, which lasted from the 1870s to about 1900. It was marked by the continued efforts to unite a country that had been divided by civil war and a huge influx of European immigration that brought religious tensions. The majority Protestant population felt threatened by this new influx of Catholics, Eastern Orthodox Christians, and Jews. Immigration also brought economic tension: The quick expansion of industry and the railroad was fueled by cheap immigrant labor, allowing those at the top to increase their wealth by an order of magnitude. People like railroad magnate Cornelius Vanderbilt were able to build mansions across the U.S.

Nannie, a young "looper" in a hosiery mill. Scotland, North Carolina, 1914. Photo by Lewis Hine.

But those immigrants, along with the still-recovering southern states, saw little to nothing of the vast economic growth their labor made possible. A PBS documentary on the period states that in 1897 the richest 1 percent in the U.S. had as much wealth as everyone else combined. As the rich were getting richer, countless others were suffering: There were two national depressions, one in 1873 and the other in 1893. People were demanding rights; labor unions were forming; child labor was challenged; women sought the vote. Partisanship was intense but national patriotism was low. Elections were close, and corruption grew as wealth was concentrated at the top. Sound familiar?

That's a glimpse into life in 1892, when Rev. Francis Bellamy was working as a staff writer for a popular Boston magazine called *The Youth's Companion*, which was owned by Daniel Sharp Ford, one of a growing number of people concerned that love of country was giving way to love of wealth. After seeing a *Boston Herald* editorial titled "The Worship of a Textile Fabric," Ford was determined to act to elevate love of country above the love of textiles.[14] To help restore the sense of patriotism, Ford enlisted his junior partner and nephew, James Upham, to start a campaign to get flags in all the classrooms around the nation. But other such campaigns hadn't gotten very far, so Ford wanted a pledge to go along with it, something that a new generation could recite daily as part of their formal education. That, he thought, could help instill loyalty and devotion to the country, and remind people that we were one, indivisible nation with noble ideals. So Ford asked Rev. Bellamy to write one.[15]

The pledge Bellamy produced was published in *The Youth's Companion* in 1892 and went like this: "I pledge allegiance to my Flag and the Republic for which it stands—one nation, indivisible—with liberty and justice for all."[16]

---

14   Francis Bellamy, "The Story of the Pledge of Allegiance to The Flag," *University of Rochester Library Bulletin*, vol. VIII, no. 2 (Winter 1953), https://rbscp.lib.rochester.edu/3418.

15   The family of James B. Upham, who was a junior partner at *The Youth's Companion*, claims that he was actually the author of the pledge rather than Francis Bellamy; they produced what they said was his original draft. The family was never successful in getting official recognition for their claim. The publication itself is no help in sorting this out because they had a policy of not listing the authors of particular pieces, letting the entire work speak for the entire staff.

16   John W. Baer, "The Pledge of Allegiance: A Short History," http://willrogers1959.com/files/Pledge_of_Allegiance.pdf. Online adaptation from the author's larger work: The Pledge of Allegiance, A Centennial History 1892–1992 (Annapolis, MD: Free State Press, 1992).

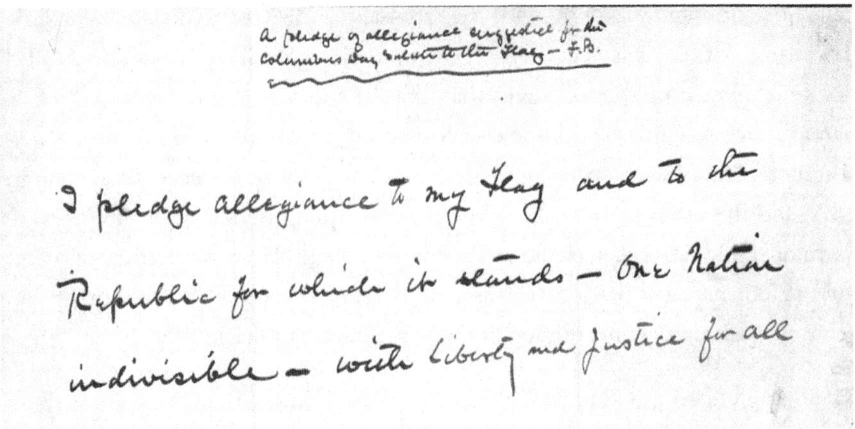

The original Pledge of Allegiance by Francis Bellamy, 1892

So far so good. But it needed a roll-out. Fortunately for Ford and his staff, 1892 was also the four hundredth anniversary of the voyage of Christopher Columbus, providing the perfect occasion to try out the new pledge everywhere. But they needed the government's permission to get it into the classrooms.

Since 1892 was an election year, and partisanship was so intense, just getting President Harrison's permission was not good enough. That would make the pledge seem partisan, so Harrison wouldn't give it a green light unless presidential contender Grover Cleveland also gave the pledge his seal of approval. With permission granted by both Harrison and Cleveland, the first mass use of Bellamy's pledge rolled out in schools across the country on October 12, 1892.[17]

Bellamy on Writing the Pledge

"That hour or more is still a vivid memory. It began as an intensive communing with the salient points of our national history, from the Declaration of Independence onwards; with the makings of the Constitution; with the expoundings of Webster; with the meaning of the Civil War; with the

• • •

---

17   Robert Longley, "Why Americans Once Gave the 'Bellamy Salute,'" *ThoughtCo.*, March 11, 2018, https://www.thoughtco.com/why-americans-gave-the-bellamy-salute-3322328.

aspirations of the people, both conscious and half-conscious, which might include the more advanced human ideas which even in those early nineties were beginning to be uttered.

Could words be found for all that? Words which the mature would understand and accept? Words which the children, if they couldn't fully appreciate, could at least feel, and might remember in afterlife? Could the words be incisive and condensed enough to lend themselves to a children's ringing shout?

At last it began to shape itself in words. Of course, start it with the main idea of the moment as the children stood at salute before the flag: "I pledge allegiance to my flag," (allegiance was the great word of the Civil War period). But why allegiance to the flag? Because the flag stands for the Republic. And what does that vast thing, the Republic, mean? It is the concise political word for the Nation, the One Nation which the Civil War was fought to prove. To make that One Nation idea clearer, we must specify that it is indivisible, as Webster and Lincoln used to repeat in their great speeches. And its future?

Just here arose the temptation of that historic slogan of the French Revolution which meant so much to Jefferson and his friends, "Liberty, equality, fraternity." No; that would be too fanciful, too many thousands of years off in realization. But we as a nation do stand square on the doctrine of liberty and justice for all. That's all any one nation can handle. So those words seemed the only roundup of past, present, and future.

Thus it was, on a midsummer evening, with a remembered sea breeze off Massachusetts Bay cooling the city, that the idea grew into shape and then into natural words. First, the attempt to get an exact vision. Then, the logical sequence of the separate thoughts, with elimination and balance. The words seemed to take care of themselves—they were the old words of American history and evolution, with the ear instinctively helping in their choice. They had been condensed to twenty-three. When they were said aloud, they seemed to have a carrying resonance together with ease of speech.

The writer went to his door and called down the hall. "Hello, there, Mr. Upham, I've got something for you to hear."[18]

---

18 Bellamy, "The Story of the Pledge of Allegiance to The Flag."

But despite that grand roll-out across the nation, the pledge still had obstacles before it could become official because Bellamy's pledge wasn't the only one out there. There was another, older pledge to the flag that was frequently used in schools and by the Daughters of the American Revolution and some other civic organizations. That other pledge had been written by Captain George T. Balch, a Civil War veteran who was also part of Upham's effort to get flags in all the schools. Balch's pledge went like this: "We give our head and hearts to God and our country; one country, one language, one flag."

With everyone now in agreement that a pledge was needed, someone had to figure out which pledge would become official. It was no small undertaking and a war intervened, so it took almost twenty years to get some action. In the meantime, some used Bellamy's pledge, others used Balch's pledge, and sometimes groups blended the two together and made their own. In the spring of 2015, we got a glimpse of just such an effort, when Emerson High School in Oklahoma City decided to replace their chalkboards and found a remarkable set of older chalkboards underneath. The older boards were from 1917 and still had intact lessons and drawings on them. One of those boards had the pledge written out for students, showing one such combination. It is pictured here and reads: "I give my head, my heart, and my life to my God and One nation indivisible with justice for all."[19]

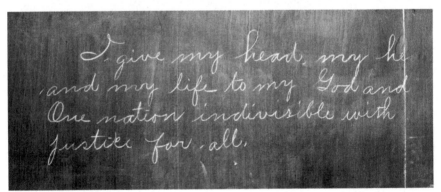

Example of variation of the Pledge of Allegiance from Oklahoma classroom, 1917

---

19   Elahe Izadi, "Haunting Chalkboard Drawings, Frozen in Time for 100 Years, Discovered in Oklahoma School," June 6, 2015, https://www.washingtonpost.com/news/morning-mix/wp/2015/06/06/eerie-chalkboard-drawings-frozen-in-time-for-100-years-discovered-in-oklahoma-school.

In 1923 more than sixty military, fraternal, patriotic, and other civic organizations, from the Boy Scouts to the American Library Association, gathered for *the* first National Flag Conference in Washington, DC. President Warren Harding addressed the group. That's where Bellamy's pledge was chosen as the pledge for public use. The organizations also tweaked the pledge in two ways. They added "of the United States" after the word "flag" ("of America" was tacked on when the Conference reconvened the following year), but the Conference also made another significant shift in the language.

Remember all those immigrants? The pace of immigration had not slowed. Anti-immigration groups began to spring up and Congress responded to pressure by enacting quotas and other restrictions on immigration in the Johnson-Reed Immigration Act of 1924. Those restrictions were almost entirely based on race and national origin, with the latter chosen with an eye to religion. Chinese immigration had been barred back in 1882, and in 1907 Japanese laborers had been added to that ban, although spouses and children of those already here were allowed. The 1924 law stopped that, blocking all Asians and other non-whites, with the exception of black Africans, and severely restricted Italians, Greeks, Poles, and Slavs, who were primarily Catholic or Jewish. The act funded deportations of those restricted groups who were already here, and when challenged in court, the only successful defense was to claim that the person was actually "white." The Office of the Historian in the U.S. Department of State lists the purpose of the act as being "to preserve the ideal of U.S. homogeneity."

These immigration battles were raging just as the Flag Conference was convening and the pledge was being codified. The result was a tiny change—so small that it's easy for us to think of it as an innocent tweak to the language. It wasn't. Bellamy's original pledge said, "I pledge allegiance to *my* flag." The majority at the Flag Conference, however, didn't like the thought of immigrants claiming the U.S. flag as their own, even if they had become citizens. So they replaced the phrase "*my* flag" with "*the* flag." Rev. Bellamy objected to that change, which the Conference duly noted—before doing it anyway.[20]

---

20 The Pledge of Allegiance—Changes Through the Years," The American Flag Foundation, Inc. Accessed May 23, 2019, http://americanflagfoundation.org/wp-content/uploads/2011/02/Official-versions-of-the-Pledge-of-Allegiance.pdf.

Front page of The Day *(New London, CT) from May 26, 1924*

SALUTE!

At the Flag Conferences of 1923 and 1924, the first Flag Code was also developed, laying out the ways the flag was to be saluted, treated, lifted, flown, and disposed of when necessary. Fast forward to the 1930s when the world stage was unsettled by the rise of both fascism and communism. In the 1930s the Nazis in Germany were rounding up Jehovah's Witnesses and sending them to concentration camps for their refusal to salute the Nazi flag.

They weren't refusing to salute because it was the Nazi flag. The Jehovah's Witnesses view the salute to any flag as a violation of the commandment against graven images. Although the Flag Conferences had included no penalties for Flag Code violations, individual states in the U.S. began to create such laws, resulting in similar issues for the Jehovah's Witnesses here. In 1935 a nine-year-old boy in Lynn, Massachusetts, was expelled and his father arrested for refusing to salute the flag. The case went to the Supreme Court in 1940, which ruled in favor of the state. In the wake of that decision, more states began adding significant penalties for failing to salute the flag.

One of those states was West Virginia, where in 1942 another family of Jehovah's Witnesses, the Barnetts, again refused to salute, resulting in the children being expelled from school and the parents brought on criminal charges. That case, too, went to the Supreme Court. But this time, the court overturned the previous decision and ruled in a 6-3 vote in favor of the Barnetts, deciding that compelling the salute was a violation of their First Amendment rights. They issued the ruling on Flag Day, 1943. The previous case was overturned in part because of the evidence of persecution against the Jehovah's Witnesses in the wake of the former ruling against them.

But the later court also had the larger world context of the persecution of Witnesses by the Nazis, whose atrocities were becoming better known every year. With movements afoot in the U.S. that were sympathetic to Nazi ideals (we'll talk about them in the next chapter), most people wanted to avoid any impression that the nation was supportive of Hitler. So we didn't want to persecute people the way they did, but that wasn't the only problem. There was an issue with the salute itself, which in 1942 was different from what we do today.

The physical salute of the flag in the United States has never changed for the military; but for civilians, it was not always placing your hand over your heart. Rev. Bellamy spelled out the physical action that should accompany the recitation of his pledge. Here are the published instructions for students:

> At a signal from the Principal the pupils, in ordered ranks, hands to the side, face the Flag. Another signal is given; every pupil gives the flag the military salute—right hand lifted, palm downward, to align with the forehead and close to it. Standing thus, all repeat together, slowly, "I pledge allegiance to my Flag and the Republic for which it stands; one Nation indivisible, with Liberty and Justice for all." At the words, "to my Flag," the right hand is extended gracefully, palm upward, toward the Flag, and remains in this gesture till the end of the affirmation; whereupon all hands immediately drop to the side.

In 1892, that kind of salute didn't seem problematic. If you stop and follow those instructions right now it actually has a nice feel to it. You salute the flag as a soldier would, and then at the words "to the flag" make what feels like a gesture of presentation. "I salute the flag and, voila! Here it is!"[21]

---

21   *The Youth's Companion*, 65 (1892): 446–447.

School children saluting the American flag using the Bellamy Salute

But if you look at the pictures of people doing the Bellamy Salute, you can see how problems cropped up once images of the Nazi salute started appearing in the media. The Nazi salute, which was also the salute of the fascist party in Italy, had the same extended arm, but with the palm down rather than palm up. Plus, Germans who refused to salute the Nazi flag were carted off to concentration camps. So the Bellamy salute began to feel a bit too close to the Nazi salute for comfort. In fact, it was close enough that photographers with bad intentions could (and did) catch the photo of the extended arm just before the palm was flipped, frame the photo so that you couldn't see the flag, and claim that the people in the picture were supporting Hitler. With just a flick of the shutter, you could falsely claim that entire schools were bringing the Nazi youth movement right into class.

In December 1942, as the Barnett case was winding its way through the courts, Congress amended the Flag Code to change the civilian salute to putting your right hand over your heart. And just six months later, the Supreme Court overturned its 1940 decision requiring the salute in school. It's hard to imagine that watching the abuse of similar laws in Hitler's regime didn't influence the court's decision to overturn its recent precedent.

But the history of the flag and its pledge doesn't stop there. By 1942 the pledge said, "I pledge allegiance to the flag of the United States of America, and to the Republic for which it stands, one Nation indivisible, with liberty and justice for all." Hmmm. . . what's missing?

UNDER GOD

Enter the McCarthy era of the 1950s. With the "Red Scare" of the Cold War, the Soviets testing an atomic bomb, the start of the Korean War, and a powerful senator picking off his political enemies by accusing them of being Communists, the nation was worked into a frenzy of fear and suspicion. It seemed like enemies were everywhere, and Senator McCarthy made sure that we turned our scrutiny not just on the nations that threatened us, but also on our fellow citizens.

It was the Knights of Columbus, the world's largest Catholic fraternal society, who started the movement to have the words "under God" inserted into the pledge; they sent a resolution to Congress in 1953. There was some support for the Knights' resolution as well as for seventeen other similar resolutions that were introduced in the House of Representatives. But none of them could muster enough votes. It took the Rev. George Docherty, a Presbyterian minister and Scottish immigrant, to push the idea over the edge.

With President Eisenhower sitting in the pews, Rev. Docherty preached a sermon pointing out that the pledge as it stood could easily be said by any little child in Moscow—in the words as they now were, there was no difference between them and us. This was a stirring argument, since Sen. McCarthy had the entire country focused on rooting out the Communists. It simply wouldn't do that our pledge could be said easily by a Soviet. Docherty had the answer. The Soviet Union was officially atheist, so no little child in Moscow could say our pledge if we added the words "under God." That did it. Congress inserted "under God" into the pledge in 1954 and it was signed into law on Flag Day that year, despite the fact that Bellamy's son and grandchildren wrote to Congress to object. As a good Baptist who believed in the separation of church and state, Bellamy would not have wanted that insertion, they insisted.[22] Again, their objection was duly noted—and ignored.

---

22   From religioustolerance.org/nat_pled1.htm. Accessed May 23, 2019.

Edward Percy Moran's painting depicts Francis Scott Key on a boat gesturing toward the American flag flying over Fort McHenry in Baltimore.

Rev. George Docherty and President Eisenhower on the morning of February 7, 1954, at the New York Avenue Presbyterian Church; the morning that Eisenhower was persuaded by Docherty that the Pledge of Allegiance must be amended to include the words, "under God."

Just two years later, in 1956, Congress enacted a law mandating that the phrase "In God We Trust" appear on U.S. currency and become the official motto of the United States of America. The phrase appears slightly differently in the fourth verse of "The Star-Spangled Banner," "Then conquer we must, when our cause it is just,/And this be our motto: 'In God is our trust.'" The phrase had also been used on some coins as early as 1864, when there was a push to show that God was on the side of the Union forces. But "In God We Trust" became universal on both paper bills and coins with the 1956 law signed by President Dwight Eisenhower—for the same reason that "under God" went into the pledge: We are not Communists!

THE NATIONAL ANTHEM

The lyrics of "The Star-Spangled Banner" were written in 1814 by U.S. lawyer Francis Scott Key and were put to the music Key asked for: a song by John Stafford Smith that was popular in Britain (an interesting combination, since the song is set during a war between the two countries). It was used officially by the Union troops during the Civil War and by the U.S. Navy starting in 1889. In 1916 President Woodrow Wilson designated Key's composition as the national anthem for all the military. It wasn't officially adopted by Congress as the national anthem of the United States until 1931. Before that, other songs like "Hail, Columbia," "My Country, 'Tis of Thee," and even "Yankee Doodle" were frequently used for civilian occasions.

Many of us learned much of the history of "The Star-Spangled Banner" in school, although not many know that what we sing today is only the first verse. The full anthem is actually a four-stanza poem of thanksgiving to God for victory at the Battle of Baltimore during the War of 1812. The events described were those that Francis Scott Key witnessed from a ship after negotiating the release of his friend, who was being held prisoner by the British. The negotiation was successful, but Key was not allowed to return to shore until the end of the battle. The Battle of Baltimore was a critical moment, since Washington, DC, had already fallen to the British, who had burned the White House, the Capitol, and the Library of Congress. If Fort McHenry hadn't been able to hold, our experiment with independence might well have been over.

Watching from the ship, Key had no way to know what would happen to his country. It was pouring rain and so a much smaller flag was flying at the fort overnight. Even when dry, the woolen flag took eleven men to hoist, so there's no way a wet woolen flag could go up. To fix the problem, they had a much smaller "storm flag" to fly in wet weather. But even with the glare from those red rockets, the storm flag was tough to see from a distance. Key had to wait until morning to see which flag flew over the fort.

> *What is that which the breeze, o'er the towering steep,*
> *As it fitfully blows, half conceals, half discloses?*
> *Now it catches the gleam of the morning's first beam,*
> *In full glory reflected now shines in the stream:*
> *'Tis the star-spangled banner! Oh long may it wave*
> *O'er the land of the free and the home of the brave!*

But there's more to the story, and it's in these undercurrents that some of today's issues around the anthem might find resonance. Key was not just

Black soldier in the British Corps of Royal Marines

any Washington lawyer. He was the consummate insider, a trusted advisor to President Andrew Jackson, who rewarded him with the office of District Attorney for the City of Washington in 1833. As racial tensions mounted in the country and the movement to abolish slavery gained momentum, both Jackson and Key sought to squash any challenge to white supremacy or to laws protecting slavery.

It's against that background that many today see the third verse of The Star-Spangled Banner as showing direct racial bias. Fighting for the British in the War of 1812 were two Marine units composed of former African slaves who had escaped the U.S. and found refuge with the British. They were known as the Corps of Colonial Marines. They played a major role at the Battle of Bladensburg, where Francis Scott Key's friend had been captured and whose release he was trying to secure the night of the Battle of Baltimore. Because of that history, many see the third verse of the anthem as a direct reference to that earlier Battle of Bladensburg and the Colonial Marines:

And where is that band who so vauntingly swore
That the havoc of war and the battle's confusion,
A home and a country, should leave us no more?
Their blood has washed out their foul footsteps' pollution.
No refuge could save the hireling and slave
From the terror of flight, or the gloom of the grave:
And the star-spangled banner in triumph doth wave,
O'er the land of the free and the home of the brave.

It's interesting to me that we sing the first verse as our anthem. While the entire poem is written from the perspective of victory, we sing the one verse where that victory is still uncertain. Unlike the anthems of many other nations, we end ours with a question rather than an affirmation: "Oh say, *does* that star-spangled banner yet wave o'er the land of the free and the home of the brave?"

The United States of Francis Scott Key and Andrew Jackson and the nation of Herbert Hoover, who signed that important question into history as our national anthem, were very different in many ways. But they are also eerily similar to each other—and to our own day. Perhaps there was some deeper wisdom afoot prompting us to select a song that ends with a piercing question as our national anthem. What flag, exactly, does fly over our nation? Do we follow its ideals? Do we change our behavior to match our values or do we change our values to match our behavior? It can be hard to see in a storm.

FLAGS IN CHURCH

To move a step closer, what flag flies over our churches? Putting our nation's flag in church sanctuaries began sporadically in the 1860s, about the same time as "In God We Trust" first appeared on coins—and for the same reasons: to force those wanting to secede from the Union to honor the flag of the United States and to equate loyalty to country with loyalty to God as a way to thwart the Confederate movement.[23]

The practice of putting flags in churches became more widespread after World War I, just as the effort to put a flag in every classroom took hold, and the practice presents us with an interesting dilemma even apart from the above history and the issues surrounding the separation of church and state. There's a much more practical problem articulated nicely by Hoyt Hickman, a staff member for the Board of Discipleship of the United Methodist Church, who responded to the question on the church website. Here's a brief summary, but you can read the whole thing by going to the link in the footnote.[24]

The core of Hickman's point is that the Flag Code requires that wherever the flag is displayed, even in a church, it must hold the position of greatest honor. In practical terms, that means if your church has a cross hanging high above,

---

23 A story about a wartime Methodist church in Missouri using the flag in this way illustrates the issue very well. It is described in a blog post by Thomas Kidd from 2016 that can be found here: https://www. thegospelcoalition.org/blogs/evangelical-history/the-church-and-the-american-flag.

24 Hoyt Hickman, "Should We Have Flags in the Church? The Christian Flag and the American Flag," https://www.umcdiscipleship.org/resources/should-we-have-flags-in-the-church-the-christian-flag-and-the-american-flag. Accessed May 23, 2019.

or even slightly above, the flag, you're in violation of the Flag Code and are dishonoring the flag. But will you really suggest putting the flag up where the cross is and sticking the cross over the right shoulder of the preacher? If you don't have a cross, will you place the flag on the middle of the altar and put the bread and wine around its base? If so, I have some commandments I'd like to show you.

When we put a flag in a church sanctuary, we are forced to either violate the Flag Code or the cornerstone of the Ten Commandments insisting that God must be given top honors. And since the sanctuary is the greatest place of honor in a church building, you can't get away with putting the flag down in the fellowship hall. That's dishonoring it as well. If you have it at all, it gets top billing: the sanctuary or bust.

So, a word to the wise. If you choose to have the U.S. flag in your sanctuary and still center worship on the cross or altar, you should be wary of any legislation to punish those who dishonor the flag. It's like Jesus said: You can't have two masters. Of course the church who chose to drape the cross in the flag as shown on the previous page came up with a different solution. It's not one I personally recommend.

THE SEVENTH-INNING STRETCH

We expect our national symbols at state and military functions, since those are national events. We've also seen them almost merge with Christianity as flags appeared in churches. But over time our national symbols have also made their way into leisure, civilian activities, most notably sports. National anthems for all countries began to be played at the Olympics starting with the 1924 games, for the same reason anthems are still played there now—as a way to both identify and honor the country of the winner in each event.

It wasn't entirely clear sailing, however, and in 1968 Queen Elizabeth's brother-in-law, Prince George William of Hanover, proposed that all national flags and anthems be removed from the games. He believed that the Olympic Games were a great unifier for the nations and that the presence of the national symbols could be a reminder of wars and tensions that had the potential to undermine the unifying spirit of the games. The prince's motion actually received majority support: The vote was thirty-four in favor of banning the symbols and just twenty-two against. But to pass it needed a two-thirds majority, which meant the motion was short by three votes. The motion failed. Prince George William resigned from the Committee and the motion was not tried again.

In the nineteenth century, the anthem was played at U.S. sporting events by military bands on special occasions, but it wasn't common. It took one war to start changing that and a second war to make it universal.

The first step came almost by accident in Chicago on September 5, 1918, at the opening game of the World Series between the Boston Red Sox and the Chicago Cubs. The U.S. had entered World War I just seventeen months before and had already lost a hundred thousand soldiers, not counting those who had come home severely wounded and traumatized. The economy was strained by the costs of war and the draft was affecting everyone, including Major League Baseball players. Why was the World Series starting September 5, you ask? Isn't it in October? Well, that year the government had ordered the regular season to end by Labor Day so that the players who had been drafted that summer could go off to war.

Opening Day at Yankee Stadium, 1923

And just one day before that game, a bombing at the Chicago Federal Building had killed four and injured thirty: That meant a severely depressed and small crowd at the ballpark for Game 1. The *Chicago Tribune* wrote the next day, "yesterday's combat between the Cubs and Red Sox was perhaps the quietest on record." But there was one part of the game that wasn't quiet: the seventh-inning stretch. A military band was usually on hand to play for sporting events, and this game was no exception. During the stretch, they decided to play "The Star-Spangled Banner."

Fred Thomas was the third baseman for the Red Sox and was only able to play because he was on furlough from the Navy to get some additional training. So when Fred heard the anthem, he did what any sailor would do and immediately faced the flag and saluted. Other players on the field did the same, which in turn inspired the crowd to start singing along. By the end of the song, everyone in the stadium was one with the anthem, which exactly expressed their fears and struggles. When the song ended, the crowd erupted into applause and cheers. Everyone from the crowd to the players to the reporters knew they had been part of a moment.

The management of both teams noticed and made sure that the anthem was played at each subsequent game. The crowds grew. By the end of the series, the song had been moved from the seventh-inning stretch to the pregame, where it was played as wounded soldiers, who'd received free tickets, were brought out onto the field for recognition. Of Game 6 the *Tribune* wrote, "Their entrance on crutches supported by their comrades evoked louder cheers than anything the athletes did on the diamond." After that series, the Red Sox made the anthem a staple of home games.

While still not universal either to baseball or other sports, the national anthem began being used more frequently during World War II to lift the spirits of the crowds. The day after the Japanese announced their surrender, bringing about the end of World War II, NFL Commissioner Elmer Layden ordered that the anthem be played at every football game, saying, "The National Anthem should be as much a part of every game as the kick-off. We must not drop it simply because the war is over. We should never forget what it stands for."[25]

As the twentieth century turned into the twenty-first, professional sports had become a multi-billion-dollar industry and the draft gave way to a volunteer military. Recruiters had to get creative to attract enough soldiers, so the physical prowess and growing celebrity of athletes seemed a perfect

25   Olivia B. Waxman, "Here's How Standing for the National Anthem Became Part of U.S. Sports Tradition," *Time*, September 25, 2017, http://time.com/4955623/history-national-anthem-sports-nfl.

pairing to a Defense Department looking to attract new recruits. The Defense Department began to push all professional sports to stage patriotic events at their games. Remember in our idolspotting lesson we learned to ask questions when there is someone at the table to discuss an issue that seems out of place? The Department of Defense at the table with a professional sport should raise some questions.

Congress took notice of these recruitment tactics and explicitly asked some of those pointed questions. On April 30, 2015, the Republican senators from Arizona, Jeff Flake and John McCain, issued a report lambasting "paid patriotism," noting that the Department of Defense had been paying for patriotic displays in football and other professional sports between 2011 and 2014. ESPN commentator Stephan A. Smith put it this way in a segment on September 14, 2016:

> The players were moved to the field during the national anthem because it was seen as a marketing strategy to make the athletes look more patriotic. The United States Department of Defense paid the National Football League $5.4 million between 2011 and 2014, and the National Guard [paid] $6.7 million between 2013 and 2015 to stage on-field patriotic ceremonies as part of military recruitment budget-line items.[26]

Our flag, anthem, and pledge come to us already tied to our racial struggles, our immigration fears, our wars, and ultimately the Christian God. These symbols entered all our classrooms, many of our churches, and all of our sporting events, sometimes paying to have added attention and focus. Our national symbols rightly deserve a very high spot on our list of priorities. But is there a chance they have taken on a bit too much power? Are they dancing with idols?

TAKING A KNEE: PREPARING FOR YOUR THIRD GROUP SESSION

In August 2016, Colin Kaepernick, the biracial quarterback for the San Francisco 49ers, refused to stand when the national anthem was played during

---

26   Greg Papke, "Stephen A. Smith Calls Out NFL Sponsored Patriotism in Light of Jerry Jones Comments," *Larry Brown Sports*, https://larrybrownsports.com/football/stephen-a-smith-nfl-patriotism/322598.

San Francisco 49ers safety Eric Reid and quarterback Colin Kaepernick kneel during the national anthem before an NFL football game against the Los Angeles Rams in Santa Clara, CA

a pre-season game. Instead, he remained seated on the bench. It wasn't the first time he had done it, but it was the time that got the most attention. When asked why he did not stand, Kaepernick responded, "I am not going to stand up to show pride in a flag for a country that oppresses black people and people of color. To me, this is bigger than football and it would be selfish on my part to look the other way. There are bodies in the street and people getting paid leave and getting away with murder."[27]

When asked to respond to Kaepernick's actions, the 49ers offered this official statement:

> The national anthem is and always will be a special part of the pregame ceremony. It is an opportunity to honor our country and reflect on the great liberties we are afforded as its citizens. In respecting such American principles as freedom of religion and freedom of expression, we recognize the right of an individual to choose and participate, or not, in our celebration of the national anthem.[28]

At the end of August, Nate Boyer, an Iraq and Afghanistan veteran with the Green Berets and a former Seattle Seahawks player, responded to Kaepernick's actions in an open letter in the *Army Times*. Boyer, who is white, expressed that Kaepernick's refusal to salute the flag would have offended him had he been standing there on the team, and then Boyer wrote the following:

> I'm not judging you for standing up for what you believe in. It's your inalienable right. What you are doing takes a lot of courage, and I'd be lying if I said I knew what it was like to walk around in your shoes. I've never had to deal with prejudice because of the color of my skin, and for me to say I can relate to what you've gone through is as ignorant as someone who's never been in a combat zone telling me they understand what it's like to go to war.[29]

After that letter was published, Kaepernick and Boyer met and arrived at a

27 Steve Wyche, "Colin Kaepernick Explains Why He Sat During National Anthem," *NFL.com*, August 28, 2016, http://www.nfl.com/news/story/0ap3000000691077/article/colin-kaepernick-explains-why-he-sat-during-national-anthem.

28 Ibid.

28 Nate Boyer, "An Open Letter to Colin Kaepernick, from a Green Beret-turned-long Snapper," *Army Times Online*, August 30, 2016, https://www.armytimes.com/opinion/2016/08/30/an-open-letter-to-colin-kaepernick-from-a-green-beret-turned-long-snapper.

middle ground. Instead of sitting, Kaepernick would kneel, as a soldier would kneel in respect at a fallen comrade's grave. That way, Kaepernick's action would be one of respect, but could also show that the U.S. had fallen short of protecting all its citizens. Kaepernick remarked that kneeling was like flying the flag at half-staff to commemorate a tragic event. It was also the posture of prayer and what players do when an injured teammate is carried off the field.

Throughout the 2016 season, a few players on various teams followed suit, kneeling rather than sitting during the anthem. But as Kaepernick received more attention, he came under criticism for the way he criticized law enforcement. A photo emerged from before his protest began when he wore socks to training camp that depicted pigs in police hats.[30] Objections to the protest merged with objections to the man. In March 2017, Kaepernick announced that he would forego the final year of his contract with the 49ers and become a free agent. No one signed him.

Although Kaepernick was gone, the protests continued at the start of the next season with the first white player, Seth DeValve of the Browns, joining in during a pregame, citing his unease with the racial hatred shown at a "Unite the Right" rally in Charlottesville in early August. In mid-September 2017, President Trump, at an Alabama rally, harshly criticized the protests, using language that many saw as racially charged. Two days after that September rally, more than two hundred players participated in the protest. The president then tweeted about it critically thirty-seven more times that September, resulting in calls to boycott NFL games where protests occurred.

Owners began meeting with players to find a way to stop the protests. Through such conversations a number of teams committed resources to help combat racial disparities in their local communities. But hate crimes were on the rise, with a 17 percent increase in 2017 over the previous year. Fifty-nine percent of those were related to race/ethnicity/ancestry.[31] While individual team efforts were a step in the right direction, the overall issue behind the protest was getting worse. The protests continued, as did the public objections to them.

---

30   Chuck Schilken, "Colin Kaepernick Says the Pigs on His Socks Were Only Meant to Represent 'Rogue Cops,'" *Los Angeles Times*, September 1, 2016, https://www.latimes.com/sports/nfl/la-sp-colin-kaepernick-socks-20160901-snap-htmlstory.html.

31   FBI, "2017 Hate Crime Statistics Released," November 13, 2018, https://www.fbi.gov/news/stories/2017-hate-crime-statistics-released-111318.

Looking for a compromise, the NFL announced a new policy in May 2018 requiring all players on the field to stand for the anthem, but giving players the right to remain off the field during that time. The owners signed on, but nobody asked the players, who rejected the new policy. The president also rejected it, and the policy was dead by July.

At the start of the 2018 season, Nike unveiled a new version of their "Just do it" ad campaign to celebrate their thirtieth anniversary.[32] Kaepernick, who had been a Nike athlete since 2011, was the central feature of the campaign. The ad showed a close-up of Kaepernick's face with the words, "Believe in something, even if it means sacrificing everything." Some responded by purchasing Nike gear—while others responded by burning the Nike gear they had and pledging to boycott the company.

The NFL responded to the ad, too. They issued the following statement:

> The National Football League believes in dialogue, understanding and unity. We embrace the role and responsibility of everyone involved with this game to promote meaningful, positive change in our communities. The social justice issues that Colin and other professional athletes have raised deserve our attention and action.[33]

Colin Kaepernick

32 Matthew Kish, "Here Are the Ads in Nike's 30th Anniversary 'Just Do It' Campaign," *Portland Business Journal*, September 4, 2018, https://www.bizjournals.com/portland/news/2018/09/04/ads-nike-30th-anniversary-just-do-it-campaign.html.

33 Around the NFL Staff, "Issues Raised by Kaepernick Deserve Attention," *NFL.com*, September 4, 2018, http://www.nfl.com/news/story/0ap3000000958222/article/nfl-issues-raised-by-kaepernick-deserve-attention.

There was still no new official policy regarding the protests. As of this writing, Colin Kaepernick and fellow protester Eric Reid remained unsigned and filed lawsuits against the NFL, accusing the league of colluding to keep them off of their teams because of their protests. The NFL settled with both men in early 2019 with terms protected by a non-disclosure agreement.[34]

With all of that attention, you might expect that the issue would grow as the 2018-19 season progressed. But it didn't. Although still at an impasse, the issue faded into the background. Why? What changed? The media companies stopped airing the national anthem in their broadcasts. Without that amplification, there were no tweets or media replays to keep up the outrage. And, just like that, the boiling pot was turned back down to simmer, heating up only at peak events like the Super Bowl or the settlement of the lawsuit.

Most people have quickly gone back to enjoying NFL games together, whether they agreed with the athletes' form of protest or not. But the intrusion of idols into the conflict has left its mark, making the sport a political football and associating our national anthem with partisanship. The battles over protesting the anthem at football games may be on the back burner for now, but the sport and the society more generally have yet to cleanse and protect themselves from the influences that could cause it to boil over again at a later time. The issues of racial injustice that were the reason for the protest in the first place remain. And the focus on the NFL has reignited debates about the professional football industry as a whole and the ways it has ignored the health and welfare of its players, the lax player penalties for domestic violence, and the outsized influence of money on the sport.

During your next group session, you will have an opportunity to discuss this issue and practice your idolspotting skills by taking a look at the various types of power that both helped and hindered the resolution of the national anthem controversy in the NFL. In preparation for that, please reflect on the following questions.

First, in order to be sure everyone is on the same page about how this all began, jot down a one-sentence response to the questions below in the space provided. The answers are all in the section above, but sometimes it's easy to

---

34   Associated Press, "Colin Kaepernick, NFL Settle Collusion Lawsuit," February 15, 2019, https://www. hollywoodreporter.com/news/colin-kaepernick-nfl-settle-collusion-lawsuit-1187235.

lose sight of the underlying issues when emotions are heated. So just make sure you're all starting from the same place by writing down a quick answer to the following to have with you for the discussion:

- What was Colin Kaepernick's reason for protesting?

- Why did he change the form of his protest from sitting to kneeling?

- How did the League respond?

- There were lots of powerful forces at work as the issue went on. Consider the list of those forces below. Are there even more you can think of? Did any one of them have a bigger influence than the others in either creating or diffusing the issue?
  - The flag and national anthem
  - The multi-billion-dollar professional football industry (each NFL franchise is worth $2.5 billion)
  - An iconic brand (Nike)
  - The president
  - Social media
  - Broadcast media
  - Celebrity players
  - Racial issues

- What should have been the primary concern for those trying to resolve the standoff? Did that issue remain central during the debate—or was it shifted to something else? If it was shifted, which of the forces above covered up the central issue?

- Who should have been the parties resolving the issue? Did any of them get pushed aside by less-central interests or powers?

- Remember the five signs of an idol's presence: Divisions are stoked, a powerful thing has inserted itself where it doesn't belong, proposed solutions are all win-lose instead of win-win, there are lies and deception about the real issue, and it's an all-or-nothing choice. Do you think any idols were at work during the most divisive time of this issue?

- Protests of all kinds are supposed to raise awareness about a problem and push those who can do something to help fix it. Do you think the NFL protests accomplished their goal of raising awareness and demanding action about racial injustice?

- Colin Kaepernick sometimes wore clothing that angered people, notably wearing socks of pigs in police hats and a shirt that showed Fidel Castro and Malcolm X in dialogue. What effect do you think such personal choices have on the larger cause for which a person is advocating?

- Celebrities in all fields have a large public platform, allowing them to quickly raise awareness on a large scale. Do you think they should use that platform to champion a cause? Are there some causes they should stay away from? For example, should they only advocate for causes within their particular industry or should they be able to take up whatever concerns them?

- As you look back on the controversy, what part(s) of it do you think Jesus would be concerned about? Are there pieces of it that match any of God's priorities?

CHECK-IN

Write a one-sentence answer to each of the following questions. You will be asked to share these with your group but without further comment:

What is one thing that was new to me in this material?

What is one question that this week's topic(s) raises for me?

SUPREMACY

How Idols Divide Us

> The greatest among you will be your servant. All who exalt themselves
> will be humbled, and all who humble themselves will be exalted.
>
> MATTHEW 23:11-12

Times of widespread injustice have historically been preceded by times of change, uncertainty, and economic pain. When we are distracted and discouraged by our own struggles, it's easy to let God's priorities slip. Over time, oppression gains ground and injustice grows, often for a decade or more, until some clear act of terror or atrocity strips away the lies that have lulled us into moral sleep. Suddenly we awaken to find that we are but a shell of what we once professed, the cancer of injustice has metastasized, and extreme measures are needed to keep our souls alive. Keeping the commandments and prioritizing the values we talked about in chapter one take courage, vigilance, and sacrifice.

We've spent a lot of time thinking about the ways that symbols can stray from their lane and pick up additional, powerful passengers that have no business being there. When a symbol of unity becomes a source of division, that's a red flag on our idol hunt. What is hiding in there and perverting the symbol? In this chapter we're going to pull the curtain all the way back to see what a few idols actually look like and examine how they divide us and how we might apply our priorities to come back together again.

Idols are false gods. They are great things that aren't content with being great. They want to be the greatest of all—they want to be God. I know I've said this a lot, but when emotions run high with some of these issues it's important to remember that labeling something as an idol isn't a smear on the thing that has been co-opted. What I'm saying is that the more powerful something is in its pure form, the more an idol would like to take it over. An invading army might gain some benefit from capturing the smaller towns, but the real power is in taking the capitol. That means the more powerful something already is, the more closely we need to guard it. Lesser things can also become infected, but the actual goal is to get into the big things and use their rightful power to stage a coup. So here we're going to look at wonderful and critically important things—the things that make up our identity as individuals and societies—and see what happens when those great things are allowed to say they are not just great, but the greatest.

Idols are boastful. Since they're not actually the greatest, they hope that by claiming they are over and over, we'll come to believe them. That makes our idolspotting a bit easier. What issues have some kind of superlative attached to them? Who or what is claiming to have not just truth but *the* truth? A superlative phrase about something that runs afoul of the priorities we examined in chapter one can tip us off to an idol lurking in the shadows, so that's where we'll be looking.

This chapter is likely to stir emotions, and I've tried to be as neutral as I can in laying out history and defining terms. You can decide for yourself whether I've succeeded. But as you read, I encourage you to remember the biblical passages and priorities in chapter one. No other gods. And the one God we are to keep in the top spot commands us to love others just as much as we love ourselves and to go about our business doing justice, loving mercy, and walking with humility. No version of "God loves me best" meets those criteria—and yet we too often make that claim with our nation, our race/ethnicity, and our faith. Buckle up.

AMERICAN EXCEPTIONALISM

The phrase "American exceptionalism" gets thrown around in both academic and political circles. Most of us know it from the latter, where candidates for public office are often quizzed about whether they *believe* in it (note the religious language), and are either embraced or shunned accordingly. "American exceptionalism" is not just the belief that the United States is a great place. It's the belief that the United States is greater than all other nations in a way that has never been and never can be replicated. We're not just a free country, for example; our freedom is stronger, better, and more protected than anywhere else. We're not just a wealthy country; we have resources that no other nation can ever hope to equal. Our founding documents are not just a good foundation for governance; there is nothing like them and, more to the point, nothing *better* than them on earth.

The concept of American exceptionalism is that whether you're talking about our military, our laws, our history, our people, our government—anything at

American Progress, by John Gast, 1872. This painting shows "Manifest Destiny," the belief that the United States should expand from the Atlantic to the Pacific Ocean.

all—we are the best. Further, that best is so good that other countries will always be playing catch-up. Our position in the world cannot be overtaken. We are special—a unique occurrence in world history that has no equal—and we make sure other countries understand that and exhibit proper deference. On the one hand, you can see how that would have appeal to those who live here. Who doesn't want to be that special? Even if you're the bottom person on the bottom rung of the national ladder, a belief in American exceptionalism still lets you feel better than Joe Schmoe from some other country. You're going to fight to keep that advantage because your self-esteem demands it.

There's also a reverse kind of American exceptionalism. There are those who say that as a country we are exceptional, yes, but we're exceptionally evil. We are wealthy because we take more than any other country and share a far lesser percentage of our wealth than any others. Our system of slavery was more cruel and repugnant than any other slave system in history. Our immigrants have made us prosperous because we have both literally and figuratively stolen from them in a way that no other country has. While the appeal on this side isn't as obvious, it's still strong. Consider this: If your identity is wrapped up in fighting for a particular cause, it's helpful to have that cause look as bleak as possible so that you can ride in and be the savior. The worse conditions are, the more you and your cause become absolutely necessary.

AMERICAN EXCEPTIONALISM GREATEST INCOME INEQUALITY . . . HIGHEST POVERTY RATE . . . GREATEST NUMBER OF CHILDREN IN POVERTY . . . WORST CHILD WELL-BEING . . . LOWEST SOCIAL MOBILITY . . . HIGHEST HEALTH CARE COSTS . . . MOST PEOPLE WITH NO HEALTH CARE . . . HIGHEST INFANT MORTALITY RATE . . . HIGHEST OBESITY RATE . . . HIGHEST ANTI-DEPRESSANT USE . . . SHORTEST LIFE-EXPECTANCY AT BIRTH . . . HIGHEST CARBON EMISSIONS . . . WORST GENDER INEQUALITY . . . HIGHEST MILITARY SPENDING . . . MOST ARMS SALES . . . HIGHEST INCARCERATION RATE . . . WORST MURDER RATE . . .

An example of the negative expression of American exceptionalism.

Both the positive and negative forms of American exceptionalism find resonance in politics, and all sides are forced to bow to some form of American exceptionalism to get elected. You can say we are the worst or you can say we are the best; you can say we need to overturn the tables to reclaim our lost crown or that we have to work hard to keep our place as the greatest nation on earth. But there is one line you can't cross if you want to succeed in U.S. politics: It's not acceptable to suggest that we team up with other nations to help everybody be equally great.

Do you recognize that? Remember the signs of an idol from the last chapter. It's the zero-sum game. Someone has to win and someone has to lose. There can be no ties, no sharing of the crown, no win-win options. It's a binary choice—first or last. And of course both the zero-sum game and the binary choice are deceptive. While we might have the greatest military in terms of size and armaments, for example, we still can be brought to our knees in an instant by a nation that can hack our power grid, even if that nation can't get a single plane off the ground. People from all over the world travel here for care in our first-rate hospitals, but many people here go bankrupt if they try to access that care for themselves. The truth is complex and nuanced. But "do you believe in American exceptionalism?" is still the litmus test for access to political power in the U.S.

Micah 6:8 says that the only thing required of us is to act justly, to love mercy, and to walk humbly with our God. There is no humility in thinking no other country can possibly be better than or even equal to us, and shouldn't be allowed to try. There is also no humility in refusing to apologize or even acknowledge our flaws when we have done harm. Loving our neighbor as ourselves isn't just about individuals, it applies to neighbor nations as well.

If we pour a bucket of humility on our exceptional nature, those claiming both the positive and negative forms of American exceptionalism might see more clearly. If there's no idol present, that humility bath frees us to see both our strengths and our weaknesses. We can acknowledge the brilliance of our nation's gifts and atone for the ugly underbelly of our flaws. But idols fight like a toddler at the prospect of bath time. If the proposal for a good dose of humility is met with antagonism, guess what? You've stepped on an idol. The antidote is not throwing the country in the trash. Don't fall for the all-or-nothing lie that idols tell. We can be a great country that still needs work in many quarters, just as wonderful people can also have significant flaws. And when another nation succeeds where perhaps we have failed, we can celebrate them and learn from them, making not just our country, but our world great.

AMERICA FIRST

Close to the idea of American exceptionalism is the phrase "America First." Just on its face, it's a natural outgrowth of the former idea. If the U.S. is truly exceptional then it's naturally first in the world. Keeping our nation first in all aspects of life is the way we defend American exceptionalism. When everything is healthy, there's nothing wrong with giving priority to our own country's needs. We expect our leaders to act, first and foremost, in the interests of the United States, and we should want everyone focused on making sure we are the best we can be in all aspects of our life together. Our policy differences largely reflect the various ways we think are the most effective to achieve that goal. There are tough decisions to be made, and sometimes even brilliant, good-hearted people get it wrong.

This Is My Song

By Lloyd Stone and Georgia Harkness
Tune: "Finlandia"

This is my song, O God of all the nations,
a song of peace for lands afar and mine;
this is my home, the country where my heart is;
here are my hopes, my dreams, my holy shrine:
but other hearts in other lands are beating
with hopes and dreams as true and high as mine.

My country's skies are bluer than the ocean,
and sunlight beams on cloverleaf and pine;
but other lands have sunlight too, and clover,
and skies are everywhere as blue as mine:
O hear my song, thou God of all the nations,
a song of peace for their land and for mine.

May truth and freedom come to every nation;
may peace abound where strife has raged so long;
that each may seek to love and build together,
a world united, righting every wrong;
a world united in its love for freedom,
proclaiming peace together in one song.[35]

---

35   Lloyd Stone and Georgia Harkness, "This Is My Song" (Lorenz Publishing Company: 1934 [stanzas 1 and 2], 1964 [stanza 3]). Admin. by Music Services. All Rights Reserved. ASCAP. Used with permission.

What I want us to examine here are not methods, but goals. I'm looking at a phrase like "America First" and seeing a potential target for idols—both because it has a desire for supremacy in its name and, maybe more importantly, because it's happened before. Our current day is not the only time that "America First" has been a national slogan. It went badly when it was first used in the 1940s. Understanding that history might help us strengthen our fortifications and keep idols at bay.

A PERSON'S A PERSON, NO MATTER HOW SMALL

Many people don't know that Dr. Seuss, whose full name was Theodor Seuss Geisel, didn't only write children's books. He also used his cartoonist skills in advertising and documentary films. From 1940 to 1943, he was the chief editorial cartoonist for a New York newspaper called *PM*, for which he drew more than four hundred political cartoons. The cartoon on the next page was drawn by Geisel and published in *PM* on October 1, 1941. As you can see from the cartoon, the phrase "America First" is not new, and it has a troubled past. Here's the backstory.

On September 4, 1940, just a year before Geisel took his position with *PM*, a Yale law school student formed the America First Committee (AFC). It was a non-partisan group that lobbied to keep the United States out of World War II. The plight of other nations, even of our closest friends, was of no concern to the AFC. Their founding statement said, "We demand that Congress refrain from war, even if England is on the verge of defeat." They believed we should take care of our own and leave the rest of the world to its own devices.

Strongest in Illinois, the AFC boasted 800,000 dues-paying members across 450 chapters at its peak, including future president Gerald Ford. Their primary funding came from Sears-Roebuck and the *Chicago Tribune* as well as individual donors. The AFC lasted just over a year, disbanding three days after the attack on Pearl Harbor in December 1941. The goal of staying out of the war was clearly not going to be achieved after that. But in the short fifteen months of its existence, the America First Committee left a controversial mark.

While there are many reasons for opposing war in general and any given war in particular, the monstrosity that was the Nazi regime in Germany heightened

... and the wolf chewed up the children and spit out their bones ... by Dr. Seuss, 1941

the intensity of the war debate. And, in providing a haven for those who opposed going to war, the AFC also provided a haven for those who opposed this particular war against the Nazis because they happened to *agree* with the Nazis that the white race was genetically superior to other races and that Jews were a problem to be eliminated.[36]

---

36 The Nazi movement, both then and now, is not just antisemitic. It has a more far-reaching racial and genetic bias, and those two things are linked. One of the underpinnings of antisemitism is the belief that the Jews are involved in a conspiracy to eliminate the white race by encouraging and aiding those of other races to settle in predominantly white areas, intermarry, and thereby dilute the "purity" of the white race. That's why white supremacists, like those who marched in the Unite the Right rally in Charlottesville in August 2017, chant "Jews will not replace us." It's why conspiracy theorists falsely claim that the people coming to the U.S. from Central America are being funded by Jewish billionaire George Soros. This will be examined more fully in another volume of this series.

The AFC was quickly charged with antisemitism and responded by booting some well-known antisemites from its ranks, including Henry Ford. The charge persisted nonetheless and then was vaulted into the limelight when Charles Lindbergh joined the group in April 1941. Bringing his fame as the aviator to achieve the first solo transatlantic flight, his gravitas as a Medal of Honor recipient, and the sympathy of a nation for the kidnapping and murder of his infant son in 1932, Lindbergh was a big draw when he held an America First rally in Des Moines, Iowa, on September 11, 1941.

Charles Lindbergh speaking at an "America First" rally in 1941

As the throngs listened, he claimed that the push for the U.S. to be involved in the war came from "the British and Jewish races," and then named the Jews as our real enemy, saying:

> "Their greatest danger to this country lies in their large ownership and influence in our motion pictures, our press, our radio, and our government."[37]

The earlier cheers from the crowd at the rally turned to boos, and it was difficult for him to finish his speech. Condemnation was swift from all quarters, but the reputation of the America First Committee as being full of antisemites and Nazi sympathizers was sealed. It didn't help that Lindbergh had been hosted by the Nazis several times in 1936 and 1938 and had received Germany's highest civilian honor, the Service Cross of the German Eagle,

---

37   Charles Lindbergh, "Des Moines Speech," September 11, 1941, http://www.charleslindbergh.com/americanfirst/speech.asp.

from the hands of Marshal Goering himself. He was encouraged to return it, as many others did with either their German or Italian awards from the period. But Lindbergh declined, donating it to the Missouri Historical Society. It was just twenty days after Lindbergh's infamous speech that Theodor Seuss Geisel published the America First cartoon above.

That speech was not an aberration for Lindbergh. His reasons for opposing the war are evident in his journal, where it's clear that he was upset not just by our entrance into the war, but also with the results. "Much of our Western culture was destroyed," he wrote. "We lost the genetic heredity formed through eons of many million lives."[38] The America First Committee of the 1940s wasn't formed for that purpose, but it was so publicly embraced by antisemites and white supremacists and did so little to disavow those messages that it came to be viewed as the home of Nazis in the U.S.. "America First" became as toxic as the swastika, even though both stood for other things before the Nazis took them over.

For our purposes, there are a couple of lessons here. First, there are many alive today who were either around in the 1940s or who know the history of that earlier "America First" movement. In my opinion, it's way too early to try to rehabilitate the phrase, even under the best of circumstances. Making that even more difficult is the fact that there is currently an America First Committee promoting neo-Nazi ideals in existence today. The Southern Poverty Law Center, which tracks hate groups across the United States, lists 121 active neo-Nazi groups as of 2017, the America First Committee among them. In other words, the association of "America First" with Nazis, racists, and antisemites is not just history. It's current events.

More to the point of our subject, the history also shows us how easily the desire to be seen as dominant—which is present in the phrase "America First"—can corrupt what otherwise can be a reasonable debate. There are always legitimate arguments about the extent to which we should be involved in conflicts abroad. There is always room for debate about what's in the national interest and how to best achieve those ends. But once you invite people to join a group, movement, or political party that promises some kind of supremacy,

---

38   Alden Whitman, "Lindbergh Says U.S. 'Lost' World War II," *The New York Times*, August 30, 1970, http://movies2.nytimes.com/books/98/09/27/specials/lindbergh-lost.html.

you have invited idols to the party. They will, given time and space, corrupt both the group and its members. The command to have no other gods is as much protection for us as it is protection for God's rightful place.

NATIONALISM

The word "nationalism" doesn't have the superlatives in its name in the way the phrases "American exceptionalism" or "America First" do. But there's a superlative present in the word's definition. According to Britannica.com, nationalism is an "ideology based on the premise that the individual's loyalty and devotion to the nation-state surpass other individual or group interests."[39] See that desire for dominance in the definition? "Surpass"? The first part—the individual's loyalty and devotion to the nation-state—is basic patriotism, although I'll throw a flag at the phrase "nation-state" in a bit. But it's really the second part—putting such loyalty above the interests of other individuals or groups—that puts it on my radar.

To understand the concern, we need to understand what a nation actually is and why we have nations in the first place. Adam and Eve didn't step out of the Garden of Eden and say, "Oh, look, we're in Iraq!" Nations were created to better manage and unify growing populations, and the earliest societies weren't large enough either to have nations or need them. Family or tribe served just fine. It was only when the population grew that more complex

---

39 *Encyclopaedia Britannica Online*, s.v. "Nationalism," accessed May 23, 2019, https://www.britannica.com/topic/nationalism.

structures were needed, and human beings responded by creating states (a given geographic area with a sovereign government) and finally nations (the shared culture, history, and ideals that connect and bond large populations together). So, roughly, a state is defined by sovereign government and a nation is defined by shared culture.

One nation can contain many "states," as in the United States. Our fifty states all have their own set borders, elect their own officials, and write their own laws within certain limits. Indian reservations are also states within a nation since they have a sovereign status within the United States, whereas U.S. territories like Puerto Rico and Guam have U.S. citizenship and protections but not the sovereign status granted to official states and Native tribes. A single state can also contain many nations, as a quick trip through most large cities across the country will show you. You can often find Chinatown, Little Italy, Little Havana, and other enclaves of people who are bound by a common heritage, language, and culture apart from the state in which they reside.

The nationalist, however, doesn't want either a nation with many states or a state with many nations. The nationalist wants a single "nation-state" where everyone conforms to a specific ideal, and where that ideal is the law. Without nationalism, the culture of a country is organically shaped from the bottom up. It's a product of the people and as the population changes, the nation adapts. Nationalists, however, want it to work the other way; they want to shape the nation from the top down—by force, if necessary.

To understand this better, it helps to look at the difference between patriotism and nationalism. Patriotism as a concept predates nationalism by about two thousand years and comes to us courtesy of ancient Rome. Patriotism has its origins in the search for the common good[40] and the belief that support of your country should lead toward freedom and justice for all. In other words, the reason we citizens should be devoted to the nation is because the nation serves the people and makes life good for everybody. Small sacrifices by us as individuals, given in service to the country, result in enormous good for all of us together. Patriotism can be expressed in military service, public service, civic engagement, or plain old hard work to keep the economy moving and

---

40 *Encyclopaedia Britannica Online*, s.v. "Patriotism," accessed April 4, 2019, https://www.britannica.com/topic/patriotism-sociology.

New Zealand military recruitment poster for World War I

thereby ensure enough for everyone. It's the complete opposite of the zero-sum game. It's not win-lose or even win-win. The service evoked by a spirit of patriotism results in a win for a nation as a whole that is even better than the win-win we get as individuals. The greatness of a nation is thereby seen in the equal welfare of all of its citizens.

Nationalism, on the other hand, harnesses those powerful expressions of patriotism, but reverses their goal. In nationalism, it is the power of the leaders to shape the nation that define its greatness. The people exist to serve the nation's leaders rather than the other way around. You might personally do well under a nationalist leader or you may fall into abject poverty, but your circumstances are not the point for the nationalist. If your dire straits are necessary for the leaders to be more powerful, then you have contributed to the greatness of the nation.

Nationalists don't use the language of "public service" to describe government workers. Instead, the nationalist complains about the "administrative state." When looking at the government, they don't see any army of patriots ready to serve. They see a large, expensive, and unnecessary bureaucracy. This makes sense when you think about it. If the nation exists to ensure the safety, freedom, and welfare of its people, the size of the government has to reflect the size of the population it serves. Got a big country with a lot of people? It takes a lot of public servants to ensure everyone has what they need. But if you think it's supposed to work the other way—that the people are supposed to serve the nation—then all those people in government are just a waste because all the citizens are there to do the work. All it takes at the top is a leader who keeps alive the vision of what the nation should be and an enforcement apparatus to keep threats to that vision at bay. The nationalist has no patience with checks to executive power—that only hinders the ability of the leader to achieve the vision. In nationalism, the important ones are at the top, not at the bottom.

Patriotism is not incompatible with nationalism. Anyone can feel devotion and loyalty to a country. Nationalism just adds a very particular vision of what that nation is. When a nationalist heart swells with patriotic fervor, that fervor is a desire for conformity to a highly defined ideal of a country. That ideal might focus on maintaining a certain geographic area, culture, race, ethnicity, language, religion, level of wealth, or some combination of those things and more. The criteria differ from nation to nation.

As a result, nationalism frequently comes with some kind of adjective that defines the values of a particular nation or movement. You can have economic nationalism, in which an individual's wealth determines whether a person fits the nation's ideal. It can be ethno-nationalism, which revolves around some combination of language, religion, or ancestral heritage. Nationalist movements in the U.S. are largely focused on race and religion, with being white and being Christian (Protestant preferred) at the center.

We'll deal with racism more fully in a later volume as well as in a variety of other issues along the way. But I want to pause briefly to distinguish between white supremacy and white nationalism, since both are relevant to this chapter and both are in the news. White supremacy is the belief that the white race is superior to all others. Frequently white supremacy contains an ethnic piece as well, with preferences for a British, Germanic, or Nordic heritage. By contrast, white nationalism is the belief that the ideal nation is only composed of white people or, if that can't be achieved, citizens belonging to other races must have a lower status and fewer freedoms. Obviously a white nationalist movement will attract white supremacists, but the white nationalists want to organize and direct the white supremacists for the creation of a nation-state made in their image. White supremacy is an ideology; white nationalism is a political movement. Sadly, the white church in the U.S. too frequently has given both groups a comfy pew in exchange for being included in that idol's power. We have barely begun to atone.

POWER CORRUPTS

Nationalism exists on the left and the right, in every religion and race, and on all continents around the world. In most cases it lives on the fringes, but when people feel insecure, for whatever reason, nationalists take that opportunity to gain power. Nationalist movements across history have followed in the wake of economic crashes, large shifts in technology that unsettle the workforce, or large displacements of people from natural disasters, famine, or war.

Once a nationalist succumbs to the idol of absolute power, they stoke rather than soothe a nation's fears, directing that inflamed fear toward the race, religion, class, or other group of people that the nationalist wants to eliminate to achieve their vision. That fear you have? That job you lost? That mouth you can't feed? It's *their* fault. You can't have your country with *them* in it. It's binary—us or them. It's zero-sum—if they benefit, you must lose. Lies are told about the suspect population, problems are exaggerated or even made up from whole cloth. Combine that message with a charismatic and dominant personality and the fringe can move quickly into the center of power. Sometimes that happens in a bloody revolution, but other times there's not much of a challenge at all. Everybody thought Hitler was crazy and no real threat—a fringe guy. Then he won, and it was too late.

Nationalism is very literally an invitation to fashion a nation in your own image. Who do you think ought to be here and who should go? Who gets privileges and freedoms and who doesn't? Where should borders start and stop? You get to decide! How convenient. Does a nationalist ever imagine a perfect nation that would exclude their own race, religion, heritage, and so on? Of course they don't, which is why I think nationalism is an open door to idolatry. Walking humbly with God doesn't lend itself to the mindset of the nationalist.

"But wait!" you say, "My ideal is that we have a truly Christian nation, without all that racism and bigotry. If we just take all those priorities from chapter one and make them the law, haven't we fulfilled the desire of the Lord's Prayer to make God's kingdom come "on earth as it is in heaven"? My response is that, while the intention may be good, every time it has been tried in the real world, the fruit has been very, very bad. It has been so bad so frequently that our Christian founders joined with our secular founders in making sure our Constitution blocked the possibility of any religion becoming established as official for the nation. We'll look at that more in-depth in the next chapter.

I believe the reason the idea doesn't work is that, as the nineteenth-century British politician Lord Acton and many others have put it, "Power tends to corrupt, and absolute power corrupts absolutely."[41] With unchecked power concentrated in a small group at the top, nationalism is much more easily

---

41   John Emerich Edward Dalberg Acton, letter to Bishop Mandell Creighton, 1887. Accessed April 25, 2019, https://www.phrases.org.uk/meanings/absolute-power-corrupts-absolutely.html.

corrupted than the structure Lincoln proclaimed that built a nation by, for, and of the people. The latter can still be twisted and captured by an idol, but such a coup is much easier in a nation-state because you only need to capture a few people to gain the whole nation. With our system of checks and balances—not just at the federal level but also including the ability of individual states to check federal power—it is much more difficult for idols to overcome them all. The kingdom of God in the Bible is presided over by God alone; even Jesus refused to accept such earthly power. I believe the church is wise to follow suit.

ONE STATE, TWO STATE, RED STATE, BLUE STATE

Nationalism may seem too big for many of us to grasp or even to do much about, but it has a smaller cousin called tribalism that virtually all of us have encountered, often in more than one form. In primitive societies the tribe might not be more than a person's extended family. In some parts of the world tribalism is characterized by religious factions; in other places it's race or ethnicity that connects tribal members. Sometimes, all of those things are overlaid on top of each other, like they are in nationalism. Tribes are just smaller versions of the same thing. In the United States today, the most divisive form of tribalism is political partisanship. You're a Republican or a Democrat, red or blue, and those party affiliations are currently strong enough in some quarters to override the bonds of family, faith, and nation.

We're all aware of whether we live in a red state or a blue state. Our social media feeds are awash in maps with the colors filled in, and the airwaves make it clear what our tribe is supposed to think about states with the other color. This is newer than many people know. Before the 2000 election, coverage on election night showed red and blue states, but which candidate was assigned red and which was assigned blue varied with each election. If anything, red was used more frequently for Democrats, following European customs that associate the color red with left-leaning politics. Playing into color-scheme politics is the memory of the blue Union uniform at a time when the northern states were typically Republican. Until 2000 you could find differing color schemes on different networks for the same election. States that went for Democrat Bill Clinton in 1996 were colored red.

It was the late Tim Russert who is often credited with accidentally changing all that on an episode of the *Today* show in October 2000.[42] With the colors already assigned for that year, Russert's prominence and the nonstop coverage before, during, and after that contentious election resulted in the NBC color scheme for that year getting stuck in our minds. Republican has been red and Democrat has been blue ever since. And once it was set in our heads, it became yet another point of division, made all the more acrimonious with an election that was awarded by the Supreme Court to the candidate who did not win the popular vote.

Things have only gotten worse. Tribalism leads to just as much violence as nationalism, and can be the precursor to wars. While there's nothing inherently wrong with belonging to a tribal group, each group has their own power structure, usually without the careful checks and balances that keep idols at bay. And political parties have not only power structures, but money. With the Supreme Court deciding in the Citizen's United case that corporations are people and money is speech, the floodgates for undue influence were opened. All that money is used to keep us divided, serving the ends of the red and blue idols put before us.

Our tribalism isn't always political, however. While sports can be a great unifier, things also can get ugly. My parents taught in a public high school, so I grew up going to all the games for all the sports. Of course we always cheered for the home team, but even as a young child I could tell that we responded to some teams differently than others. The football rivalry for the Thanksgiving Day game was strong, and tensions were higher then. Basketball always seemed pretty friendly, but hockey games were downright dangerous. When we played one particular town in hockey, there was always violence outside after the game. People were thrown over cars, fistfights broke out, and general ugliness reigned—and that was suburbia with two all-white teams.

---

42 Ben Zimmer, "Thinking about Tim Russert, Red States and Blue States," *Visual Thesaurus*, https://www. visualthesaurus.com/cm/wordroutes/thinking-about-tim-russert-red-states-and-blue-states.

Somehow it was more than winning or losing. Fans stuck with their tribe and a loss was treated like an existential threat.

As an adult, when I lived in the home of the Florida Gators, I witnessed firsthand the transformation of good people who attended my church when they donned the orange and blue and went to a game. I remember one church member proudly telling me about going with her husband to a football game against the Georgia Bulldogs. The Gators lost that game and the couple returned to their car feeling sullen. My parishioner told me, with a gleam in her eye, that a Bulldogs fan came up to their Gator-bedecked car, looked into their open car window and started barking, mocking the Gator loss. She added, with smug satisfaction, that her husband, who also was in church every week, grabbed the guy by his tie, rolled up the window and began to drive away as the man, still attached to his tie, ran to keep from falling or choking. After a few feet her husband let go, but I never quite got over the glee of my fellow church member boasting of an assault over a football game.

We have our tribes in the church, too. Some are called denominations, others are just called churches with various names, symbols, and traditions. The problem is probably best described by an old joke about people from Church A who are in heaven getting a tour of the place from St. Peter. As they approach one particular section of heaven, St. Peter tells them to be very, very quiet as they pass by. "Why?" asks a person from Church A. "What's going on?"

"They're from Church B," St. Peter explains. "They think they're the only ones here."

Whichever church, denomination, or tradition we belong to, there are others who believe that we don't deserve God's favor or a place in heaven. They and only they have the truth. And, chances are, our own church or denomination passes similar judgments. We just make the inhabitants of heaven and hell pack up and move to the opposite place. While those divisions exist in almost every religion, I want to stick here to the divisions within the Christian faith: Christians claiming that other professed Christians are beyond God's mercy. That's the tribalism I know best.

Christian tribalism is not an example of being humble. Jesus is always encouraging us to self-reflection, to find the logs in our own eyes before telling others that they have a speck in theirs. (Matthew 7:3–5) We are supposed to look for our own sin before casting stones. (John 8:7) Yes, we are told to call each other to account, but in an environment more like an AA meeting and less like a courtroom. We are all sinners here. When we believe someone has left the Christian path, love and humility are the only approaches that fit within our chapter-one priorities.

If you're not sure whether a particular division in the church is legitimate or fueled by an idol, remember your basic idolspotting skills:

- **Is the fruit bad?** That is, can the various sides talk reasonably with each other or does hatred and fighting weaken the overall witness of the church? Is there spiritual, emotional, or physical violence? Threats? Incitement? Is the spirit of the law being broken to adhere to the letter of the law? One obvious example of bad fruit can be seen in the Protestant/Catholic divides that have terrorized England, Scotland, and Ireland for hundreds of years with wars, desecrations, and bombings. Throw in the Spanish Inquisition, the Salem witch trials, and targeted killings of abortion providers, black Christians, LGBT Christians, and so on, and you've got some really rotten fruit.

- **Does the point of division get more attention than it should?** I think questions around sexual orientation are the perfect illustration for this point. My own United Methodist denomination is facing schism over this as I write. If you count up all the times this issue is mentioned in the Bible, you don't even need to take off your shoes. Jesus doesn't mention it at all, despite the fact that various sexual orientations existed in both Old and New Testament times.

  By contrast, issues around money and possessions get more than five hundred verses in the Gospels alone. But sexual orientation is what we're splitting the church over? We have somehow evolved so far in our Christian walk that we can now start to examine whether the wrong people are loving each other? We'll be looking at all the issues surrounding sexuality when we get to the adultery commandment, but I see in this the example of an idol at work. Our attention to sexual orientation is way out of proportion to its miniscule importance in the Bible. Something else is going on here.

- **Do you see a zero-sum game going on?** Are you being told that giving something to someone else will somehow mean less for you? Read through Jesus' parable about the workers in the vineyard in Matthew 20:1–16. The owner of the vineyard hires people throughout the day and negotiates the pay at the point each person is hired. Everyone is fine with their offer until the pay is handed out at the end of the day and the people who worked ten hours got the same as those who worked one hour. The people are angry. The owner responds, "Are you envious because I am generous?"

That parable isn't told in the context of labor laws. It begins with the phrase, "for the kingdom of heaven is like. . . " and it ends with "So the last will be first, and the first will be last." The parable asks the angry workers as well as those of us who share that anger, "So what did you lose exactly?" I've found one thing church folks have little tolerance for is God's generosity; unless of course they are the one being given the gift. Suggest that God's love might just be broad enough to allow those of other faiths into heaven and you can feel the tension in the room. Or you can replace another faith with any particular group that your own tribe happens to believe lies outside of God's mercy. How does God's love for them mean less love for you, exactly? That's zero-sum thinking, and it's the sign of an idol at work.

• **Are there lies, deception, or binary choices?** I'm combining these last two idolspotting signs because one of the near universal lies of an idol is that we only have a binary choice: all or nothing. Abortion is a good example. When you're looking to see if an idol is blocking progress, you check out the position of each tribe and the way they each frame the issue. Is it all or nothing? Does it have to be either all evil or all perfectly fine? Whichever side you're on, does your side kick out people who try to take a nuanced position? Those nuanced positions are the bridges where dialogue can be found, which is exactly why idols don't want them around. Division is the name of the game, because division is the only way an idol gets to keep the power it has usurped.

So whether it's social issues like abortion or strictly church issues like forms of baptism, styles of worship, rituals around Holy Communion, church polity, and so on, idols must block dialogue at all costs. Real conversation might allow some prophet in the group to remind people about God's true priorities and knock Humpty Dumpty off the wall. So the idol throws out lies, distractions, and the fear that if you give even an inch to the other side, they will trample you underfoot and all you hold dear will lie dead in the mud.

Perhaps the sneakiest form of the binary choice is the lie that if there is an idol present, it's only on one side—*their* side. *They* are the ones who are deceived by a false god. *We* are the ones who see clearly. Ahem. That lack of humility is a tip-off. Chances are, when an issue has gone off the rails and sent people into warring tribes, there are warring idols pushing *each* side. There will be no resolution until we can take the logs out of our own eyes, and put the idol back in its place.

Again, that doesn't mean the idol's proper place isn't an important one. Don't buy into the all-or-nothing lie. Saying that an idol is at work is not the same as saying that the thing that became an idol should be eliminated. To go back to our example of the smoking controversy in chapter two, once money was exposed as the idol of the tobacco companies, the answer was not to forbid corporations to make a profit. The answer was to put public health and safety back as the top value and move money back to its proper role in service to those goals. In another example, we can take pride in our ancestry without issue as long as it doesn't puff itself up to make us think that our own heritage makes us better than those who are different.

Remember that a thing becomes an idol because of the way it functions, not because of what it is. When we spot an idol, it's the function we have to address, not the thing itself. Humility is what repurposes an idol and clears the way for both justice and mercy.

THAT'S THE SPIRIT: PREPARING FOR YOUR FOURTH GROUP SESSION

In 1981 my husband and I celebrated our honeymoon with a trip to Iceland where we took a week-long camping tour to some of the remote places on the island. Our group included people from quite a few countries, but my husband and I were the only ones from the U.S. One day, on a particularly long drive, our tour guide asked each of us to come to the microphone and sing something that represented our own country. When our turn came, we had a hard time. Every time we started into a song, someone else on the bus would interrupt and tell us it wasn't a U.S. song. "No, that's German." "That's a French song." "That comes from Africa." So we turned it back on them. "Okay, then," I said. "You tell us. What song represents our country to you?" Someone on the bus began to sing, "Daisy, Daisy, give me your answer, do. I'm half crazy, all for the love of you. . ." Almost everyone on that bus knew the song and we all sang it together.

Couple seated on an 1886-model quadracycle for two in front
of the south portico of the White House, Washington, D.C.

Ironically, that song wasn't from the U.S. either. It was written by a British songwriter and was first performed in London in the 1890s. But it caught fire in the U.S. and was broadly known here. And somehow, to this group of many nations, it had almost universally come to fit their image of this country—a couple in love, unable to afford a stylish wedding, but content to give up the fancy carriage and simply ride a bicycle built for two. The song speaks of optimism, adaptability, and the desire to seek unexpected solutions, values that many might call our national spirit.

For two chapters now we have talked about the symbols of the United States and some of the divisions we experience in defining who we are as a nation. The ideas about what the United States stands for are often shaped unconsciously by the culture in which we grew up. Our identity is shaped by the stories our parents read to us, the movies and television shows we watch, the songs we sing, and the way U.S. history is framed in the schools, churches, and civic celebrations we attend throughout our lives.

As you get ready for your next group session, I invite you to think about how you might describe "our national spirit" to someone who didn't know much about the United States. How would you describe what our citizens, at their best, are like? What are the values that shape us? What parts of our history explain us? What would you tell this stranger to watch or read to get a sense of the country? Where would you encourage them to visit? What song would you sing?

You'll want those thoughts kept fresh for when you meet, so please consider the following questions and write down at least one answer for each. Responses don't have to represent the ideal—just things that speak to who we are, whether you see that as positive, negative, or neutral.

- Where should a tourist visit to better understand and/or appreciate this country?

- What events in our history shaped us as a nation?

- In each of the following categories, what is at least one thing that would help a stranger get a sense of the U.S. and its people? Answers can be things from the past or present and don't have originated here.
  - TV shows (including miniseries)
  - Movies/theater
  - Books
  - Graphic art
  - Music

- The following are all iconic figures in U.S. culture drawn from art, history, and folklore. Pick three that resonate with your own sense of the country. You can also pick someone or something not on the list.

  - Lone Ranger/Tonto
  - Rosie the Riveter
  - John Henry
  - Paul Bunyan
  - Susan B. Anthony
  - Luke Skywalker/Princess Leia
  - Pecos Bill
  - Miles Standish
  - Johnny Appleseed
  - White Buffalo Woman
  - Brer Rabbit/Brer Fox
  - Batman/Robin
  - Jim Crow

  - Davy Crockett
  - Frank Drebin
  - Shane
  - Harriet Tubman
  - G.I. Joe
  - Dilbert
  - Long John Silver
  - Huck Finn/Jim
  - Bonnie and Clyde
  - Archie and Edith Bunker
  - Andy Taylor/Barney Fife
  - Pocahontas
  - Scarlett O'Hara

- What are the characteristics of the nation's spirit as you see it? What are the attitudes, behaviors, and values that sum up the essence of this country?"

- Finish this sentence: I hope that the United States . . .

CHECK-IN

Write a one-sentence answer to each of the following questions. You will be asked to share these with your group but without further comment:

What is one thing that was new to me in this material?

What is one question that this week's topic(s) raises for me?

FREEDOM

The Bulwark Against Idolatry

At least in popular rhetoric, freedom is the primary value in the United States. There's a reason that the note we hold the longest and that soars the highest in the national anthem occurs with the word "free." As values go, I don't think a secular nation could select a better one. In my reading of the Bible, freedom seems to be the central right that God works to protect. From the minute that God gave Adam and Eve the freedom to be disobedient and eat the fruit to the moment God allowed human beings to nail Jesus to a cross, human freedom appears to be the one thing that God will not violate, no matter how much we abuse it. I believe that is closely tied to the truth of 1 John 4:8, which tells us "God is love." Love becomes something else entirely if it isn't freely chosen, making freedom the necessary condition for love and second only to love itself in its power.

If you want to displace love, you have to at least severely hobble freedom, which makes freedom movements as well as laws designed to protect freedoms a prime target for idols. These efforts can be very hard to spot, but they exist on the left and the right, in all countries, and across time. And once you sign on to a freedom-based cause, it's difficult to see what's happening around you, because now they're your tribe. But remember the signs. Look for bad fruit and deception (even if it's only small at first). Listen to the language that claims it's all or nothing. Is even the slightest suggested check or critique met with, "Why do you hate freedom?" A deli near my house still sells "freedom fries," a holdover from a surge of anti-French sentiment during the George W. Bush presidency, when the French expressed opposition to U.S. policies in Iraq. How do you know if cries for freedom have been infected with idols? Renaming your french fries because someone said torture is bad is a pretty solid clue.

Look for signs of the priorities from chapter one: love of neighbor, doing justice, loving mercy, walking humbly. The fewer you see of those, the more likely it is that there's a problem. To dethrone love, an idol first needs to bend the public understanding of freedom to serve its own needs. There are constant efforts to do just that. But we have to be careful not to throw the baby out with the bathwater. Just because the bathwater becomes polluted with an idol, doesn't mean the baby isn't precious.

A very recent example of an attack by an idol on freedom is the targeting of the Black Lives Matter movement by the Internet Research Agency, the Russian troll farm indicted by Special Counsel Robert Mueller. The metaphorical "baby" in this instance is a member-led organization seeking to "build local power and to intervene in violence inflicted on Black communities by the state and vigilantes."[43] Black Lives Matter is a type of freedom movement, raising the cry that when people are killing you because of your race and the country shrugs its shoulders, you're not free in very fundamental ways. As the movement gained momentum, the Russians swooped in to discredit it in a sweeping social media campaign—a campaign that also had secondary goals of suppressing the black vote in the 2016 election, deepening the divide between the black community and police, and sowing distrust of the media.[44]

Even without well-funded, state-sponsored idols, good-faith attempts to protect freedom can be truly challenging. To begin with, we often don't recognize when freedom is under siege. We think freedom is doing just fine because we feel free ourselves, but we often fail to look around to see if that feeling is true for everyone. In other cases we have difficulty finding the delicate balance between freedom and law, a paradoxical struggle that crops up in St. Paul's letters a number of times, especially in the book of Galatians. To have a free society, there has to be a bargain that we will limit some of our personal freedoms for the sake of the common good.

For a simple example, unless a critical mass of people is willing to give up their right to drive like a bat out of hell on the roads and follow a basic set of traffic

---

43 Accessed May 23, 2019, https://blacklivesmatter.com/about.

44 April Glaser, "Russian Trolls Were Obsessed with Black Lives Matter" *Slate*, May 11, 2018, https://slate.com/technology/2018/05/russian-trolls-are-obsessed-with-black-lives-matter.html.

laws, none of us are free to focus on the more important issues we face; we're too busy trying not to die on the way to work. That's yet another reason why all justice is social justice—we all need to participate to make it work for everyone. If it doesn't work the same way for everyone, it's not justice; it's privilege.

**If it doesn't work the same way for everyone,
it's not justice; it's privilege.**

The U.S. Constitution, with all its checks and balances, tries to walk that delicate line, hoping that just enough law can allow freedom to ring with clarity across the land. As a nation, we all have to walk that tightrope every day. A woman once said to Benjamin Franklin, "Well, Doctor, what have we got? A republic or a monarchy?" Dr. Franklin replied, "A republic, if you can keep it."[45] Our founders had just come out of a bloody revolution to free themselves from the tyranny of King George, so they knew firsthand the kinds of liberties that could be at risk in a nation with a king. In response, they tried to craft a Constitution that would protect the country from those abuses. But that Constitution depends on citizens who are actively engaged in keeping it.

Our faith and our highest values are the same way. The biblical vision of justice we imagined in chapter one doesn't just happen. Every time I pray, "Thy kingdom come, thy will be done on earth as it is in heaven," I can almost hear God saying, "Are you doing your part to make that happen?" If we share God's priorities, we have to work to keep them, and freedom is key to the work of protecting both the church and the republic. Whether you're inside or outside any given religion, if love is your highest priority, the pillars of freedom must be guarded at all costs. When freedom falls, the idol wins. The assault on those pillars has taken similar forms across time and nations, most frequently in the attempt to abolish the lines between the power of religion and the authority of a nation.

---

45   Attribution found online at Bartleby.com. Accessed April 26, 2019, https://www.bartleby.com/73/1593.html.

SEPARATION OF CHURCH AND STATE

In the United States, church and state are a flirtatious couple, with one set of friends encouraging them to get married and another set of friends warning them that they are not right for each other. Of course that debate isn't new, and it isn't unique to the United States. We can go all the way back to the God-kings of the ancient world to see the natural tendency to merge human and divine authority. Histories just as old also show us the openings for human rights abuses such a merger creates.

Church graphic for Independence Day sermon

By now you've thought enough about idols to realize the dangers of taking perhaps the two most powerful institutions in the world—nations and organized religions—and making them one thing. I have never met a human being, myself included, who could safely navigate that union and keep idols at bay. In the last chapter we remembered Lord Acton's famous words, "Power tends to corrupt and absolute power corrupts absolutely." A lesser known quote of his says, "Everybody likes to get as much power as circumstances allow, and nobody will vote for a self-denying ordinance." While I wish it weren't so, I agree with both of those statements. So in this chapter we'll look at the way our founders tried to protect us from ourselves, the higher standard to which the Bible calls us, and the places where idols manage to gain influence anyway the minute we take our eye off the ball.

In seven countries today—Yemen, Sudan, Saudi Arabia, Mauritania, Iran, and Afghanistan—the connection of religion to the political power of the state is direct and intentional. That is also true in Vatican City, which operates as a sovereign city-state. But there are groups in other countries who also would like a state religion. This is true of Zionists in Israel, but we don't only need to look abroad. Here in the United States, Christian Reconstructionists, Christian Dominionists, and a group called "The Fellowship" (which runs the National Prayer Breakfast) would like to see the United States eliminate the establishment clause of the Constitution and officially become a Christian nation. So why don't we? If most of our founders were Christians, why did they put up a block to a Christian nation in our Constitution? Glad you asked.

Every Thanksgiving we remember, sometimes with tensions, that a ship called the Mayflower came to the shores of Cape Cod in 1620. While not all passengers came for religious reasons, almost half of them were Christians fleeing religious persecution. Those Puritan "Separatists," or Pilgrims as we came to call them, had already fled from England to Holland, but the economic situation was so dire in Holland that they signed up to take a chance in this New World they had heard about. We have learned about their journey and their trials upon arrival with varying degrees of accuracy in U.S. schools and museums.[46]

As the surviving passengers formed a colony and developed a government, they were eager to make sure their faith was protected, as you might expect. That wasn't really a problem in the small Plymouth Colony. But when a second and much larger wave of English Puritans showed up on these shores and formed the Massachusetts Bay Colony a decade later, their first governor, John Winthrop, employed the biblical vision of a "city upon a hill" to make the Puritan version of reformed, Calvinistic Protestantism the law. By 1691 the Pilgrims of the smaller Plymouth Colony had been absorbed into Massachusetts Bay and by 1692 the larger colony was burning "witches" in Salem.[47]

---

46 If you want both a great read and a pretty accurate description of what happened, you could do a lot worse than Nathaniel Philbrick's bestseller, *Mayflower: A Story of Courage, Community, and War* (Penguin Books, 2007).

47 For more on the Puritanism of Massachusetts Bay, see this article: https://www.khanacademy.org/ humanities/us-history/colonial-america/colonial-north-america/a/puritan-new-england-massachusetts-bay. For more on the difference between the Puritans and the Pilgrims, see Richard Howland Maxwell's "Pilgrim and Puritan: A Delicate Distinction," found here: https://pilgrimhall.org/pdf/Pilgrim_Puritan_A_Delicate_Distinction.pdf.

There were many different kinds of Puritans, just as today there are many kinds of Baptists, and some of those different kinds of Puritans were mixed together in Massachusetts Bay, including the Separatists from Plymouth Colony we now call Pilgrims. But there were others as well, all part of the general reform movement that sought to "purify" the Church of England by simplifying the rituals and using the Bible rather than church hierarchy as the final authority. In the language we used in the last chapter, Puritanism had its own tribes, and they didn't always get along.

One of those who ran afoul of the Puritan tribe in power in Massachusetts Bay was a Puritan minister named Roger Williams. One of his objections was that he didn't think people should be punished for violating the "first table" of the Ten Commandments—basically the religious codes. For example, Williams thought it was fine to punish murderers and thieves (part of the "second table"), but he believed people should be free to follow their conscience when it came to how strictly to keep the Sabbath or to decide what constituted a "graven image." Williams also had political concerns about the way the colony was governed. But since church and state were the same thing, taking issue with the way the colony conducted its affairs was also a religious offense allowing punishment from both religious and state authorities to be levied against it.

Engraved print depicting Roger Williams, founder of Rhode Island, meeting with Narragansetts, 1856

The colony was not happy about his lax approach to some of the Ten Commandments, but what eventually got Roger Williams expelled from his pulpit and from Massachusetts Bay entirely was his belief that the Indians were not being treated fairly by the colony. Rev. Williams studied the tribal languages, made friends among the Wampanoag, and organized the first attempt to prohibit slavery in any of the British American colonies. But what really got him in trouble was when he started challenging the seizure of land by royal charters without proper compensation to the tribes.

Williams went back to England for a bit to try to get that changed, and even went so far as calling King James (the king who commissioned the King James Version of the Bible) a liar when he claimed to be Christian while treating the Native peoples unjustly. This rarely goes over well with kings, and James was no exception. The unjust seizures kept happening and Williams kept objecting and soon he was convicted by the court in Massachusetts Bay of sedition and heresy and had to make a run for it.

Helped by the Wampanoags and Chief Massasoit along the way, Roger Williams was able to escape Massachusetts Bay, and in 1636, with the help of the Narragansett tribe further south, he established a settlement he called "Providence." The eventual Colony of Rhode Island and Providence Plantations was strictly a civil government, with Williams insisting that there be what he called a "wall of separation" between church and state and that Rhode Island hold fast to principles of full religious liberty and freedom of conscience. As a result, both the first Baptist church (which Williams founded with John Clarke) and the first Jewish synagogue in the United States can be found in Rhode Island. More than a hundred years later, as the colonies became a separate nation, our founders agreed with the wisdom of Roger Williams that both church and state were better protected when Williams's "wall of separation" between the two was maintained.

THE CONSTITUTION AND BILL OF RIGHTS

As the U.S. Constitution was being drafted at the Constitutional Convention in 1787, a number of delegates wanted to include a bill of rights that would offer those same protections and more. Many knew the benefits of the English bill of rights, in place since 1689, and there were also several individual states who

already had adopted their own bills of rights. One of those states was Virginia. George Mason, who was a Virginia delegate to the Constitutional Convention, proposed that they not go home until a federal bill of rights had been added to the new U.S. Constitution.

Maybe they were just tired after four long months of deliberations, or maybe they thought it wasn't all that necessary. But whatever the reason, the state delegations unanimously voted down the resolution to add a bill of rights. George Mason and two other delegates refused to sign on to the new Constitution because of that omission, and the Convention finished without any protections for religion or speech. Without the Bill of Rights, the only mention of religion in the Constitution comes in Article VI, provision 3: "No religious Test shall ever be required as a Qualification to any Office or public Trust under the United States." God is not once mentioned or implied from start to finish.

Although the convention approved it, the new Constitution couldn't take effect until at least nine of the thirteen colonies had ratified it. George Mason must have shown a wry smile as the absence of a bill of rights became a major sticking point in those ratification votes. Enough colonies objected to that omission that they could only get to the nine votes needed by promising that a bill of rights would be added as quickly as possible after ratification. Once the ratification of the Constitution was complete in 1788, with four colonies still withholding votes, James Madison, who had also been a Virginia delegate and who would become the fourth U.S. president, went to work on a new federal bill of rights. He used the Virginia bill of rights as a template and referenced other suggestions submitted by the states.

Since the Constitution itself was already ratified, the items in the Bill of Rights were listed as amendments, each of which had to be ratified separately. Madison drafted nineteen of them. The House of Representatives cut that down to seventeen and the Senate cut it to twelve, and those dozen amendments went to the states for approval in 1789. Everybody was on board except Rhode Island, which still wasn't satisfied, believing there was too much compromise on the issues of slavery and the control of currency. Once neighboring states threatened to cut Rhode Island off commercially, they signed in 1790. Ratification in Rhode Island passed by only two votes, but at last all thirteen colonies were part of the new republic. The states finally approved ten of the twelve amendments by December 15, 1791, and the job was done.[48] They did a pretty good job. The U.S. Constitution is the oldest written constitution still in use across the world.[49]

The Constitution and its amendments comprise a wonderful and powerful document. But, as you know by now, good things with great power require watching, since they can easily become the targets of power-hungry idols and slide into corruption. Our founders knew this, making a system of checks and balances a necessary part of the government, but Madison gave us an additional layer of protections in the Bill of Rights. In the many writings of his that have come down to us, we can see his reasoning. A deeply religious man, James Madison knew all too well how easily corruption takes hold in both the church and the state. In a 1774 letter to Philadelphia attorney William Bradford Jr. he wrote of the church, "Ecclesiastical establishments tend to great ignorance and corruption, all of which facilitate the execution of mischievous projects."[50] The problems of the church are not new.

But Madison didn't lay all the blame on the church. In 1787 he wrote, "The essence of Government is power; and power, lodged as it must in human hands, will ever be liable to abuse."[51] On July 10, 1822, he put those ideas

---

48 One of the remaining two later became the Twenty-seventh Amendment, which is the most recent amendment to be ratified.

49 "This Day in History, June 21, 1788: U.S. Constitution Ratified," The History Channel, accessed May 23, 2019, https://www.history.com/this-day-in-history/u-s-constitution-ratified.

50 Letter from James Madison to William Bradford, 24 January 1774, *Founders Online*, National Archive, accessed April 26, 2019, https://founders.archives.gov/documents/Madison/01-01-02-0029.

51 Bill of Rights Institute, accessed April 26, 2019, https://billofrightsinstitute.org/educate/educator-resources/founders/james-madison.

together in a letter to Edward Livingston, who was then a congressional representative from Louisiana's first district, where Madison defended the separation of church and state this way:

> Notwithstanding the general progress made within the two last centuries in favour of this branch of [religious] liberty, & the full establishment of it, in some parts of our Country, there remains in others a strong bias toward the old error, that without some sort of alliance or coalition between Gov' & Religion neither can be duly supported: Such indeed is the tendency to such a coalition, and such its corrupting influence on both the parties, that the danger cannot be too carefully guarded agst . . . . Every new & successful example therefore of a perfect separation between ecclesiastical and civil matters, is of importance. And I have no doubt that every new example, will succeed, as every past one has done, in shewing that religion & Gov will both exist in greater purity, the less they are mixed together.[52]

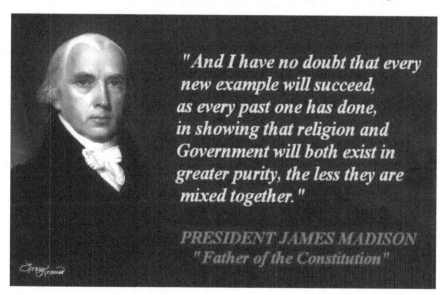

"And I have no doubt that every new example will succeed, as every past one has done, in showing that religion and Government will both exist in greater purity, the less they are mixed together."

PRESIDENT JAMES MADISON
"Father of the Constitution"

While the process of producing the United States Constitution and Bill of Rights managed to keep idols from taking hold, Madison was keenly aware that there were still powerful forces that would like to co-opt the power of both religion and the government for their own ends. To combine them would

---

52 Letter from James Madison to Edward Livingston, 10 July 1822, *Founders Online*, National Archive, accessed April 26, 2019, https://founders.archives.gov/documents/Madison/04-02-02-0471.

be to create a power so close to absolute that it would be unable to resist the temptation of trying to take God's place, sacrificing faith, the republic, and the land of justice that both seek to achieve in the process. James Madison issued warnings and kept watch, something that is needed in every age.

As we are hunting idols today, and those idols lurking near the Constitution in particular, we should watch when protections listed in the Bill of Rights take on a life apart from the rest of the Constitution and become associated with revolutionary movements, special interest groups, and partisan conflict. They might be legitimately working to protect our freedoms. But we would be fools not to heed Madison's warnings and keep watch for bad fruit and the other signs of trouble. Idols looking to make a power grab love to breathe division into the freedoms designed to protect us. Once we turn on each other and take our eyes off the ball, idols can make their move unnoticed. So where do we start?

I don't think there's any current social unrest over the Third Amendment, which prohibits quartering a soldier in a person's house without permission, although the world is crazy enough right now that we shouldn't laugh it off. Amendments nine and ten just give instructions on how to handle issues when there are no instructions. All quiet on that front as well. Amendments four through eight deal with rights about search and seizure and various aspects of processing and prosecuting legal cases. There is a lot of discontent there, but those issues fit better with other commandments and will come later in this series. The First and Second Amendments, however, are currently sucking a lot of oxygen out of the room and are leaving a lot of bad fruit in their wake, so that's where we're going to focus in this volume: the First Amendment in this chapter and the Second in the next.

FIRST AMENDMENT

Amendment I

Congress shall make no law respecting an establishment of religion, or prohibiting the free exercise thereof; or abridging the freedom of speech, or of the press; or the right of the people peaceably to assemble, and to petition the government for a redress of grievances.

The First Amendment has a lot of protections in it—religion, speech, the press, assembly, protest—it's all there. We've already looked at protest back in chapter two, to which assembly is partially related. Freedom of the press will be highlighted when we talk about false witness in a later volume. Here, we'll take a look at the two remaining: freedom of speech and freedom of religion.

FREE SPEECH

In the United States we are guaranteed the right to free speech without infringement from the government. We are not, however, guaranteed the right to be free from the consequences of our speech and, in some cases, it's still possible for our speech to break the law. For example, you're technically free to lie under oath in a legal proceeding. No one can force you to tell the truth, and there's actually another amendment (the fifth) that allows you to just be silent if telling the truth would incriminate you. But if you decide to ignore all that and lie anyway, you have perjured yourself and committed a crime. Keeping the system of justice functioning for everyone overrides the right of any individual to just say, without consequence, whatever they want in a legal proceeding. It's that delicate dance of law and freedom again.

It's also illegal for a corporation to lie about its products. False labels and claims can land a company in court. In October 2016, the company My

Pillow paid over a million dollars to settle a lawsuit brought for false claims about medical benefits that had not been tested; about claims that inventor Michael Lindell was a "sleep expert," though he had no specific training to back that up; and about using the approval of the National Sleep Foundation as a marketing ploy—when in fact the NSF was financially connected to the business.[53] Companies get hit with these kinds of charges all the time. Though they're allowed to be generally misleading—for instance, you can name your cereal "Robust Health Flakes," even if there's not a healthy ingredient in it—you can't claim to be "recommended by health experts nationwide" unless you have an independent, scientific study to back up your claim.

While protection from fraudulent claims on products protects consumers, there are no protections at all for something I think is at least equally important: It's perfectly legal for politicians to lie. In April 2016, the Supreme Court ruled in *Susan B. Anthony List v. Driehaus* that it was legal for political candidates to lie, striking down an Ohio law against it. So today candidates for public office can lie, campaigns can lie, as can all those who create ads and campaign materials on their behalf. They can't lie to Congress or to law enforcement, but to us voters it's open season, and no state can pass a law to hold them accountable.

Further, since the court ruled in that case on the basis of free speech, political

53   Ben Guarino, "Infomercial Sleeper 'My Pillow' Gets $1 Million Wake-up Call over False Medical Claims." *Washington Post*, November 3, 2016, https://www.washingtonpost.com/news/morning-mix/wp/2016/11/03/infomercial-sensation-my-pillow-gets-1-million-wake-up-call-over-false-medical-claims.

media also can lie. That further compounded the problems from the 2010 ruling of the Supreme Court in the Citizen's United case, which held that corporations are people and money is speech. Put the two cases together and media organizations can spend as much as they want to spread their message—which doesn't have to be true—as far and wide as they wish. It's now up to the voters to sort it all out; something we don't seem particularly adept at doing. You might remember that the ninth commandment forbids bearing false witness, but church and state are separate entities, so breaking the Law of Moses does not break the laws of the United States.

Those broader questions of truth-telling will come with that commandment later in the series, but it's worth pointing out that our First Amendment freedoms come with some heavy responsibilities for all who care about justice. After all, our concern for justice makes it illegal to lie under oath. Our legal system knows that if a person can't be held accountable for telling the truth, there can be no justice. Our entire system depends on it. Yet those who are elected to oversee our justice system—in Congress, in the executive branch, and even the judges and attorneys general themselves can get themselves into those positions through lies and deceit, legally amplified by millions of dollars in corporate media advertising or social media propaganda. Justice literally depends on every voter paying attention, fact-checking, and doing all they can to find out if a candidate's claims are true.

But before you get enraged, realize that the same freedom that allows a political candidate to lie also allows undercover investigators to lie. In Iowa there was a law making it a crime to lie about why you wanted to access an agricultural facility. In January 2019, that law was struck down in a federal court as a violation of the First Amendment.[54] Those laws were put on the books in Iowa and elsewhere after a number of undercover investigations turned up cases of severe animal abuse and food safety issues that prompted large-scale meat and egg recalls. Corporations don't like having their bottom line take a hit like that, so they pressured lawmakers into passing laws making such investigations more difficult. The Supreme Court threw a free-speech flag at those laws. It takes similar kinds of lies to investigate hiring or housing

---

54   Esha Bhandari, "Court Rules 'Ag-Gag' Law Criminalizing Undercover Reporting Violates the First Amendment," ACLU, January 22, 2019, https://www.aclu.org/blog/free-speech/freedom-press/court-rules-ag-gag-law-criminalizing-undercover-reporting-violates.

discrimination and to infiltrate gangs, terror cells, and trafficking rings. Do we really want that ability shut down?

Another tricky issue involves inflammatory speech. You can get up before a group and say all kinds of ugly and hateful things without fear of legal prosecution. The crowd can boo you off stage, as they did with Charles Lindbergh, and a private employer can hear about it and fire you for violating the company's values, but your speech can't be charged as a criminal matter, with one exception. If that speech is designed to threaten, incite people to violence, or otherwise cause physical harm, you can be charged.

The classic example is that you can't yell "Fire!" in a crowded theater when there is no fire, just to disrupt the place. People can be crushed and killed running for the exits, making your speech a threat to public safety; you can be charged for that. But when it comes specifically to hate speech, the courts have had difficulty finding the line for what constitutes incitement to violence. How direct and specific do your words have to be? There have been at least six cases about this brought to the Supreme Court since 1919, with the latest one in 1969. That last case, *Brandenburg v. Ohio*, involved a speaker at a Ku Klux Klan rally and concerned an event in 1964.

Ohio law at the time said that advocating violence made you a part of a criminal syndicate and was a chargeable offense. So when speakers at the rural Ohio rally called for revenge against Negroes (their word wasn't as kind), Jews, and any who supported them; accused the president, Congress, and the courts of suppressing the white race; and announced plans for a march on Washington on the Fourth of July, the Klan leader, Clarence Brandenburg, was charged. Brandenburg appealed and the case made its way up to the Supreme Court.

The Court reversed Brandenburg's conviction and ruled that, to be a crime, the speech has to be "directed to inciting or producing imminent lawless action and is likely to incite or produce such action." That ruling overturned one earlier action by the Supreme Court and called four others into question. Those who hear the words, and especially those who are the target of the hate, may understand the intention full well. But "it's obvious" is not a legal defense. If the court can't draw a direct line to violent acts close to that time or if it doesn't seem to the court that violence was caused by the speech, people can get away with saying what they want.

That can be infuriating when we can see full well the harm being done, but it's also easy to see how stricter interpretations could be abused. Martin Luther King Jr. was accused of inciting violence and famously even came under FBI investigation under the old laws. Most of those who speak out passionately about their concerns could find themselves sued or jailed by opponents of their cause if their freedom to speak is not protected. These things cut both ways.

New technologies also raise new questions about free speech, especially with government officials and agencies having a presence on social media. A federal judge in New York ruled on May 23, 2018, that it's unconstitutional for the president to block U.S. citizens on Twitter, ruling that such blocks constituted unlawful censorship by "suppressing speech on the basis of viewpoint." And what constitutes a threat on social media? If someone gets mad and responds to a post saying, "Watch your back, you [expletive]. I know where you live," how can you tell if that message is "likely to incite or produce" a lawless action or if it's just some deranged person mouthing off? It seems only a matter of time before issues like that get to the high Court.

But apart from what is legal regarding our speech, the rulings for speech in the church come from a higher and more restrictive court. The Bible has some pretty strong feelings about words. In Genesis, God created the universe through speech. "God said . . . and there was . . . ." The Gospel according to John claims that the Word became flesh and lived among us. The book of Proverbs is full of praise for the tongue of the wise and warnings about the tongue of the wicked. It's all summed up nicely in James 3:6: "And the tongue is a fire. The tongue is placed among our members as a world of iniquity; it stains the whole body, sets on fire the cycle of nature, and is itself set on fire by hell." Turn on the news or head to social media any day of the week and you will find fiery tongues staining the body, loudly and without shame. Christians ought to be especially wary of the way speech is used in our public life, starting—as we always should—with our own.

Unless you're Quakers, speech plays a primary role in every service of worship. There's a reason many churches put the pulpit both front and center. We preach, we respond, we sing words, we greet one another, we read words aloud from the Bible, we speak prayers to God, we announce church business. Knowing the creative power of words from Genesis and the subsequent warnings in Scripture about the power of the tongue, people of faith should be the most careful guardians of our own speech on the planet. But we're not.

Merriam-Webster defines hate speech as, "Speech that is intended to insult, offend, or intimidate a person because of some trait (as race, religion, sexual orientation, national origin, or disability)."[55] We expect to be held accountable for our behavior in church. Keeping us on the path to justice has always been a key role of the prophet, and we should always make a path for that voice, as uncomfortable as it can be to hear. But there's a difference between speech that calls us to account for our own actions and speech that stealthily turns us away from ourselves to lay blame on broad categories of others.

Hate speech flows freely from too many pulpits and other Christian institutions, often broadcast over the airwaves. There are places where it is blatant and public, like the Westboro Baptist Church. There are other places where it attempts to hide behind a flimsy veil of warning against damnation.

---

55 *Merriam-Webster*, s.v. "hate speech (n.)," accessed April 26, 2019, https://www.merriam-webster.com/dictionary/hate%20speech.

Yes, it happens in other faiths too, but this is about taking the logs out of our own eyes and most of the people reading this are Christians who claim "love your neighbor" as part of the Great Commandment and humility as one of the primary things the Lord requires. Hate speech is bad fruit.

Remember this: God is love. If anyone comes away from a sermon, prayer, or other element of a church service feeling less loved than before, if any group of people has been cast as anything less than God's beloved, if church members march out into the world to fight against a group of people rather than to achieve justice for a group of people, then in my view God has not been allowed to speak. Just because the laws of the United States let us do it, doesn't mean that the law of Love Your Neighbor lets us off the hook.

Churches should also watch the ways their space is used. Many churches, struggling to make ends meet, often rent their space to other groups or share it with other congregations. In your rental agreement, do you have terms that would prohibit hate speech within your walls? Does your church even have a definition of hate speech to provide to potential users? Christians should be very concerned about hate speech, and most especially about churches and religious institutions that practice it. Our God-given right to freedom includes the right to be free from verbal intimidation and abuse. Jesus himself warns us: As you've done unto the least of these, you've done it unto me. It's bad enough when hate speech comes from the secular world. When it comes from those who have taken the name of Jesus in baptism or otherwise call themselves the people of God, they are taking God's name in vain.

> **"If anyone thinks he is religious and does not bridle his tongue but deceives his heart, this person's religion is worthless."**
>
> JAMES 1:26

When we keep watch over our tongues, we help ourselves as well as others. The full version of the commandment about idolatry includes the following phrase in Exodus 20:5, "I the LORD your God am a jealous God, punishing children for the iniquity of parents, to the third and the fourth generation of those who reject me." That sounds really unfair, if you take it as literally God's desire to punish those who had nothing to do with the sin. But if you read it as stating that sin sends its hurtful tentacles down through the generations, then it's simply an expression of a psychological truth that is evident in many of our churches. Abuse left unaddressed can affect the church and its people for generations.

Churches that may not currently tolerate hate within their walls often need to confront ugly parts of their past before they can thrive. But that can be really hard to do, and those who do it have to be willing to sacrifice. For example, many churches sit on land that was stolen from Native tribes long ago. I once sat in a conference session of my own United Methodist denomination during which we had a long, moving worship service of repentance for our history as a church of abusing Native peoples, including confiscating their land for our churches.

Just a day later, still at that same conference, we closed a congregation and voted that the church building and land—land that had once belonged to a local Native tribe—be sold. What was done with the money? Was it given back to the tribe to help atone for the harm we had just spent several hours repenting of the day before? That possibility didn't even come up. The money went right back into our own coffers. We have no business repenting if we don't really mean to make amends, and those we ask for forgiveness can tell if our words are empty.

A positive example comes from a Baptist congregation in New Orleans who had to face down a history of cross-burnings and the fact that the literal cornerstone of their building was laid by the KKK in 1923. Almost a hundred years later, their ministry was stifled in a way they couldn't understand. No amount of legitimate desire for racial integration in the modern-day congregation and no amount of outreach or even staffing diversity had allowed them to grow and be in real ministry in their community. Nothing worked. Sitting in the middle of a large city, they couldn't grow.

Ku Klux Klansmen join the congregation of the Massay Line Church of God, located near Birmingham, Alabama

Then the pastor had the nerve to go to an elderly parishioner to see if the old stories were true. Had the church really burned crosses in the sanctuary? What about that cornerstone? Was the Klan really involved? The answer was yes, and the larger community knew it. Before they could move forward, the church had to go back there and find a way to repent of the hate that once was allowed to fill their sanctuary, literally, with fiery tongues. Raising the issue woke the hate that still remained within the congregation; the entire process was hard. But their solution and the public repudiation of their past finally healed the wound and allowed the church to grow and thrive after decades of decline.[56] Their earlier sin had indeed harmed the church for three to four generations. It blocked the witness of that church until they could confront the idol that was literally carved into their cornerstone. With the hateful idol identified and repudiated in public, the path to justice and full ministry within the city opened once more.

RELIGIOUS FREEDOM

When it comes to religion, the First Amendment deals with two related points: "Congress shall make no law respecting an establishment of religion, or prohibiting the free exercise thereof." The first section is called the "Establishment Clause" and the second is called the "Exercise Clause." James Madison, who wrote those words, was an Anglican who was deeply

---

56   Eric Reed, "Uncovering My Church's Ku Klux Klan Connections," *Christianity Today*, Spring 2005, https://www.christianitytoday.com/pastors/2005/spring/my-churchs-ku-klux-klan-connections.html.

distressed by the religious persecution he witnessed in the colonies. Before he ever got to drafting the Bill of Rights for the country, he made sure that his colony of Virginia had its own protections for the free exercise of religion as Rhode Island and several others had done much earlier. It took him eleven years to get his bill through the Virginia legislature.

Madison wrote extensively on the necessity of keeping church and state separate, as we've seen. But he was clear-eyed about the challenges and acknowledged that it was a work in progress. In a letter to Rev. Jasper Adams in the spring of 1832, Madison wrote:

Freedom of Religion

Establishment Clause
Congress shall make no law repescting the establishment of religion.

Exercise Clause
Prohibits government from unduly interfering with the free exercise of religion.

> It may not be easy, in every possible case, to trace the line of separation between the rights of religion and the Civil authority with such distinctness as to avoid collisions and doubts on unessential points. The tendency to a usurpation on one side or the other, or to a corrupting coalition or alliance between them, will be best guarded agst by an entire abstinence of the Govt from interference in any way whatsoever, beyond the necessity of preserving public order and protecting each sect agst trespasses on its legal rights by others.[57]

He was right; it isn't easy to find the lines, which is why freedom of religion cases head to our courts on a regular basis. But the principle itself was so important to him that it's the first thing mentioned in the very first amendment that he wrote. I'm emphasizing this because it's clear from his other writing that this didn't spring merely from the practical concerns of governing or even from a general concern for human welfare. It was rooted in his own Christian faith:

> Whilst we assert for ourselves a freedom to embrace, to profess and observe the Religion which we believe to be of divine origin, we cannot deny equal

---

57 Letter from James Madison to Rev. Jasper Adams, January 1, 1832, accessed April 26, 2019, https://www.goodreads.com/quotes/146772-it-may-not-be-easy-in-every-possible-case-to

freedom to those whose minds have not yet yielded to the evidence which has convinced us. If this freedom be abused, it is an offense against God, not against man: To God, therefore, not to man, must an account of it be rendered.[58]

I have exposed my inner Madison fangirl to make the point that, just as with Roger Williams, there is a strong Christian case to be made for religious tolerance and ensuring that no government agency can discriminate on the basis of religion. In the history of our nation Christians fleeing persecution played a pivotal role. And yet it is frequently Christians, including some of those earliest Pilgrims, who forget our own trials and lead the charge to remove religious protections from others. In what we've come to call the Golden Rule, Jesus said, "Do to others as you would have them do to you." (Luke 6:31, NIV) We ignore that pretty regularly.

In our current period, as antagonists whip up sentiment against Islam, at least seven states have passed laws forbidding Sharia law from being applied by the government. All but sixteen states have at least considered it. But those pushing such laws don't just want to stop Islam from controlling the government; they want specifically to ban the practices of Muslims who adhere to Sharia and to have the courts enforce that ban.

Both things are already prohibited by the First Amendment. Neither a state nor the federal government can establish any religion as civil law under the Establishment Clause, so all those laws banning the state from adopting Sharia are a waste of ink. It's already there in the Constitution. You can't establish Islam; you can't establish Judaism; you can't establish Christianity or any other religion. And it's also in the Constitution that all religions, not just Christianity, are free to practice their faith under the Exercise Clause. If members of a mosque want to hold their members accountable to Sharia, they're allowed to do that under the Exercise Clause, as long as the practice doesn't violate U.S. law.

But it's tricky, as Madison noted, so the federal government passed the Federal Arbitration Act in 1925, which allows any religion to basically set up their own courts to judge on religious matters specific to their own faith. The decisions reached by those religious tribunals are given the weight of law in state and

---

58 Leonard W. Levy, *Treason Against God: A History of the Offense of Blasphemy* (New York: Schocken Books, 1981), xii.

federal courts. Such religious courts exist even within religions. The United Methodist Church has a Judicial Council that makes such decisions. If a member of the United Methodist clergy is defrocked by the Judicial Council, the state will no longer recognize him or her as a valid officiant at weddings, for example. The Catholic Church has its own system of tribunals that has been the source of contention when dealing with the clergy sex abuse scandals. The Orthodox have one, as do the Anglicans, the Presbyterians, and the Amish. There is a Jewish one called a *beth din*. Islam has courts as well.

All those religious courts settle questions of religious law within the confines of the U.S. legal system. So, for example, a Christian court can't mandate a literal enforcement of "an eye for an eye," no matter how much they think that injunction should be literally applied, because poking out someone's eye in revenge is against U.S. law. And if people believe a religious court is not treating them fairly, they can take their case to a regular civil or criminal court. That's what is beginning to happen with the sex abuse cases, as more and more Catholics sense that their own system is not providing justice regarding that issue. Those religious tribunals are not one religion imposing anything on another; it's the U.S. government recognizing a decision about religion by that religion's own authority. It's the freedom to exercise your religion, within the bounds of U.S. law, whether Jew, Christian, Muslim, or anything else. All that has stood up to the tests of the First Amendment.

> "The door of the Free Exercise Clause stands tightly closed against any government regulation of religious beliefs as such. Government may neither compel affirmation of a repugnant belief, nor penalize or discriminate against individuals or groups because they hold views abhorrent to the authorities."
>
> WILLIAM J. BRENNAN

As with speech, however, our freedom to exercise our religion isn't without boundaries. If my religion calls for child sacrifice, the government can step in and stop me. But let's say my religion is hateful but not violent. If someone wants to form the Aryan Nation Church of All White People and require DNA tests of anyone who seeks to become a member, they can do that. They just have to meet the criteria of a church under U.S. law. Even so, however, those Aryan Nation Church members are not free to discriminate outside of that church setting. They can't run a public restaurant and refuse to serve people of color. Church members can't refuse to provide legal government services, medical care, or anything else to people based on their religious beliefs.

A clear case of how this works comes to us from Kentucky, where a county clerk named Kim Davis refused to issue marriage licenses to same-sex couples following the Supreme Court's marriage equality ruling in June 2015. She cited her personal, religious objections to marriage for same-sex couples as the reason for her refusal. The problem for Ms. Davis was that she was not refusing, for example, the use of her church for a same-sex wedding. That would have been protected under the Exercise Clause because it would involve a religious decision about a religious ceremony. But that wasn't the case. Ms. Davis was employed by the county government and was refusing to comply with the law which she swore to uphold when elected to that position. The Exercise Clause only applies where it does not conflict with the nation's laws. She could refuse to conduct such a ceremony, because that was not a requirement of her job. But she couldn't refuse to give a license to those who were qualified under the law to marry.

There are some places where the law makes specific exceptions for religious belief. A person can opt out of paying into Social Security on religious grounds (which also means you can't collect in retirement). During times of the military draft you could be a conscientious objector if your faith practiced pacifism. But unless the law names a specific religious exemption, you have to follow the laws of the United States if you live here, even if you find them objectionable on religious grounds. And that's clearly the case if you, like Kim Davis, hold government office and take an oath to uphold those laws. Which is not to say she didn't try.

To attempt to get around the charge, Ms. Davis stopped her office from issuing marriage licenses altogether. If she couldn't refuse to issue licenses to same-sex couples, she argued, then she wouldn't give marriage licenses to anyone. Predictably, that went to court, and she was ordered to begin issuing marriage licenses to all qualified couples. When she refused, she was jailed for five days for contempt of court. The state legislature resolved the standoff by passing a law that no longer required the names of county clerks on marriage licenses, but the court ordered Kentucky to pay the attorney's fees for the four couples (gay and straight) who were part of the lawsuit. In November 2018, Kim Davis lost her re-election bid.[59]

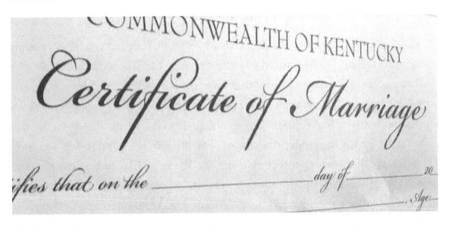

While the Davis case was clear enough that higher courts declined even to hear the case, other situations are murkier. Hobby Lobby is a private, for-profit business owned by the Green family. The family has a religious objection to contraception and in 2012 sued the Department of Health and Human Services, which mandated through the Affordable Care Act that businesses offer insurance plans that include contraceptive coverage. Since the business pays in part for the coverage for employees, they argued that they should be exempt from that part of the law. In a 5-4 ruling, the Supreme Court ruled that the exemptions for non-profit organizations could apply to for-profit corporations, although they limited the decision to only the objection to contraceptive coverage.[60]

But what about cakes? In 2012, a gay couple who married in Massachusetts sought to celebrate in Colorado and went to the Masterpiece Cakeshop to get a cake for the occasion. The owner refused to serve them, citing his

59   Associated Press, "Kentucky Clerk Kim Davis May Have Hefty Legal Bill in Gay Marriage Case," NBC News Online, Jan. 31, 2019, https://www.nbcnews.com/feature/nbc-out/kentucky-clerk-kim-davis-may-have-hefty-legal-bill-gay-n965301.

60   *Burwell v. Hobby Lobby Stores*, Oyez Online, accessed April 26, 2019, https://www.oyez.org/cases/2013/13-354.

religious objection to same-sex marriage. Colorado has a state law forbidding discrimination on the basis of sexual orientation, so the couple took them to court. The lower courts ruled in favor of the couple, starting with the Colorado Civil Rights Commission. But the Supreme Court overturned those decisions in 2018 in a 7-2 ruling.[61]

If you were just reading the headlines, that decision—especially the vote margin—was baffling. Why were liberal justices supporting the bakery? When you read the decision, it turns out it was because the Colorado Civil Rights Commission showed hostility, not just to the religion of the cakeshop owner, but to religious concerns more broadly. Justice Kennedy, in writing for the majority, said, "At several points during its meeting, commissioners endorsed the view that religious beliefs cannot legitimately be carried into the public sphere or commercial domain, implying that religious beliefs and persons are less than fully welcome in Colorado's business community."[62] In other words, the decision never addressed the big picture about whether the bakery could discriminate on the basis of religion. It decided instead that the Colorado commission, which had first ruled against the bakery, had shown enough hostility toward the religion of the bakery owners that they could not guarantee that the lower court cases had been decided fairly.

To emphasize that this was not to be interpreted as permission to discriminate, even in selling cakes, Justice Kennedy went on to say, "The outcome of cases like this in other circumstances must await further elaboration in the courts, all in the context of recognizing that these disputes must be resolved with tolerance, without undue disrespect to sincere religious beliefs, and without subjecting gay persons to indignities when they seek goods and services in an open market."[63]

In that opinion, Justice Kennedy is trying to walk the tightrope that Madison envisioned. In order to be truly free to exercise our religion, we have to be free from hostility toward our religion from governing authorities, whether our religion is deemed misguided or not. The courts may still rule against our

---

61   Masterpiece Cakeshop, Ltd. v. Colorado Civil Rights Commission, 584 U.S. ___ (2018).

62   Ibid.

63   Robert Barnes, "Supreme Court Rules in Favor of Baker Who Would Not Make Wedding Cake for Gay Couple," *Washington Post*, June 4, 2018, https://www.washingtonpost.com/politics/courts_law/supreme-court-rules-in-favor-of-baker-who-would-not-make-wedding-cake-for-gay-couple/2018/06/04/50c68cf8-6802-11e8-bea7-c8eb28bc52b1_story.html.

Lydia Macy, 17, left, and Mira Gottlieb, 16, of Berkeley, CA, rally outside of the Supreme Court which is hearing the 'Masterpiece Cakeshop v Colorado Civil Rights Commission,' case Tuesday, December 5, 2017

religiously based actions, as they did with Kim Davis. Justice Kennedy's written opinion indicates the Supreme Court might have ruled against the cakeshop if the Colorado commission hadn't been so hostile. But he is emphasizing that if our case is not treated with understanding and respect for the sincere beliefs motivating our actions—however much the law, society, or a given judge might differ—then justice is not done. It's what "do justly, love mercy, and walk humbly with your God" looks like. Under the careful words of the Bill of Rights, religious people can't force their beliefs and practices on civil society, but neither can civil society spit in the face of religious belief or prevent the religious from peaceably practicing what they believe under the law.

While U.S. history gives us a lot of thought and examples for how these concepts play out, it's worth going back to a much earlier point in history to see how Christians from other ages have handled the inevitable clash between their faith and the laws under which they live in general society. This is an age-old question, because what we do for a living is not immaterial to religious life. Faith is not a leisure activity; it's a way of seeing and being in the world. If our faith does not spill over into the way we conduct ourselves at work, we can't really say we hold real beliefs at all but only intellectual opinions.

But Christians during the first centuries after Christ had a strikingly different approach to professions they found to be in violation of their moral code than we do in the U.S. today. They didn't take the job and work to shape it in a way that reflected their values like we try to do. A second-century Kim Davis would not have tried to use her office to force her beliefs on others. She would have quit her job when the law changed to require actions that she could not in good conscience perform.

Eberhard Arnold in *The Early Christians: In Their Own Words* writes,

> The rank afforded by property and profession was recognized to be incompatible with [Christian] fellowship and simplicity, and repugnant to it. For that reason alone, the early Christians had an aversion to any high judicial position and commissions in the army. They found it impossible to take responsibility for any penalty or imprisonment, any disfranchisement, any judgment over life or death, or the execution of any death sentence pronounced by martial or criminal courts. Other trades and professions were out of the question because they were connected with idolatry or immorality. Christians therefore had to be prepared to give up their occupations. The resulting threat of hunger was no less frightening than violent death by martyrdom.[64]

Some of those other professions included theater and teaching because both included promotion of the Roman or Greek gods. The first known conscientious objector to military service was a Christian named Maximilianus, who was drafted into the Roman army in the year 295. He refused to serve due to his religious beliefs. He was executed for that response, and we now know him as Saint Maximilian as a result.[65]

These decisions were not easy, as Eberhard describes. It meant extreme financial hardship in many cases, and sometimes, as with Maximilianus, death. But the earliest Christians saw their calling as focused on molding their own behavior to match that of Jesus rather than on trying to force a change in the behavior of others whose beliefs were different. They believed that a

---

64   Eberhard Arnold, *The Early Christians: In Their Own Words*, 4th ed. (Farmington, PA: The Plough Publishing House, 1997), 15–16.

65   "Conscientious Objection to Military Service," The Office of the United Nations High Commissioner for Human Rights (2012), https://www.ohchr.org/Documents/Publications/ConscientiousObjection_en.pdf.

Ο ΑΓΙΟΣ   ΚΩΝΣΤΑΝΤΙΝΟΣ·   Η ΑΓΙΑ   ΕΛ

Icon of Saints Constantine and Helena in Dormition
of the Mother of God Church, Filipovo

lasting change in society would come not from the top down, but from the bottom up, energizing them to share the Gospel and add to the number of believers. That is totally compatible with the way God has Moses introduce the Ten Commandments to the people. That code of behavior was presented as voluntary. God had just freed them from coercion and offered a different path—the option of loving relationship and a freely chosen way of life that would make that relationship blossom and flourish.

Of course Christian history has examples of the opposite kind of approach, notably when one of those who came to believe the Gospel happened to be the Emperor Constantine in the early fourth century. This is also a very simplified version of a complex history, but pretty much all of the things those first Christians found antithetical to Christian behavior were part of the job of being emperor, and when Christianity was established as the religion of the empire, two things happened.

On the one hand, the state embrace of the faith stopped the persecution of Christians and allowed Christian churches and institutions to flourish. On the other hand, now that Christianity was joined with the wealth of an empire and belonging to the sanctioned religion determined access to political and military power, it was only a matter of time before idols took control. Wars, inquisitions, and corruption followed. And only some forms of Christian belief and practice were allowed. By the sixteenth century, the Protestant reformers' attempts at cleaning up the corruption were not welcomed, and new persecutions began. Then Protestants took hold of political power in some countries, established their religion, and the same cycle began anew.

Before Christians demand that public schools teach faith as they see it or pass laws to enforce one view of Christian practice, we should revisit our history all the way back to a hill called Mt. Calvary, where the Roman state executed a Jewish rabbi who claimed his kingdom was not of this world. Jesus could have led a revolution and overthrown that state. He could have accepted Satan's temptation in the wilderness to be the ruler of all the earth. But he chose a different path. His earliest followers did also, becoming known for their acts of mercy and generosity.

But when earthly power came knocking, doors opened and the hands of Christ became stained with blood and corrupted by gold. Centuries later a group of dissenters chafed under that rule in England and set sail for a new land where they could live their faith freely, as we saw at the beginning of this chapter.

When Roger Williams established the State of Rhode Island and Providence Plantations as a place where religious freedom could be enshrined into law, he didn't just mean freedom for various Christian sects. As he wrote in his 1664 book *The Bloudy Tenent, of Persecution, for cause of Conscience, Discussed, in A Conference betweene Truth and Peace*: "It is the will and command of God that, since the coming of his Sonne the Lord Jesus, a permission of the most Paganish, Jewish, Turkish, or Antichristian consciences and worships, bee granted to all men in all Nations and Countries."[66]

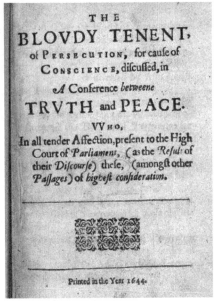

Title page of The Bloudy Tenent by Roger Williams, 1644

Massachusetts Bay tried to conquer Rhode Island, marching on its towns to try to re-establish its hold on religion. Because it was still more than a century before the American Revolution, Rhode Island's continued existence depended on the protection of the English king—now Charles II—and Parliament. So Williams got on a boat to make his case. Of course if England had been open to religious freedom, you wouldn't have had Massachusetts Bay in the first place, so Williams had an uphill battle. Nobody in England thought religious freedom (or "Soul Libertie" as Williams called it) was a good idea.

But against all odds, Roger Williams convinced King Charles that Rhode Island was far enough away from England to try an experiment with a new way for both church and state to thrive in the Colonies. Williams won over the king, and in granting the Rhode Island Colony the right to practice the religion of their choice, Charles II of England became the first monarch in history to

---

66 Accessed April 26, 2019, http://press-pubs.uchicago.edu/founders/documents/amendI_religions4.html.

grant the full freedom of religion.[67] The experiment was so successful that later charters from the king for both New Jersey and Carolina also assured religious freedom. (A *Smithsonian Magazine* article on Williams and his efforts is worth your time. The link is in the note.[68])

What Roger Williams fought for and won and what our founders agreed with so strongly that it became the first item in our Bill of Rights should not be idly tossed aside. Where religion is free, individuals can become as engaged as they wish in promoting their beliefs and persuading others to join them. But where religion is law, persuasion becomes coercion and we all lose not only our freedom but any legitimate claim to be the people of God. When church and state are joined, the new entity is an idol and we take God's name in vain.

MONUMENTAL DECISIONS: PREPARING FOR YOUR FIFTH GROUP SESSION

On June 2, 1913, commencement day, a new statue was unveiled at the University of North Carolina at Chapel Hill. Atop a tall pedestal was a carving of a young man in the uniform of the Confederacy, his presence the results of a years-long push by the United Daughters of the Confederacy to erect a monument in honor of Chapel Hill students who left school "and joined our Southern Army in defense of our State." All told there were about 1,000 students and employees of the university who left to join the war, and 287 lost their lives. The lad on the statue became known as "Silent Sam" because he had no ammunition on his belt, part of a tradition of "silent sentinel" monuments erected in both the North and the South to commemorate the common soldiers who fought for one side or the other in the Civil War.[69] Silent Sam was actually modeled after a young man from Boston.

---

67   Accessed May 23, 2019, http://sos.ri.gov/divisions/Civics-And-Education/teacher-resources/rhode-island-charter.

68   John M. Barry, "God, Government and William Rogers' Big Idea," *Smithsonian Magazine*, Jan. 2012.

69   Chris Carola, "Civil War 'Silent Sentinels' Remain Quiet Memorials to the Common Soldier," *The Christian Science Monitor*, April 18, 2015, https://www.csmonitor.com/USA/2015/0418/Civil-War-Silent-Sentinels-remain-quiet-memorials-to-the-common-soldier.

Silent Sam monument at the University of North Carolina, Chapel Hill

Before we look more at this statue specifically, it's worth noting that the vast majority of monuments erected, named for, or dedicated to the memory of the Confederacy were done either in the four decades that spanned the creation of the Jim Crow era (1890–1930) or in the aftermath of the 1954 decision in *Brown v. Board of Education* to integrate public schools. Just coincidence? Many suspect that most Confederate memorials were intended to be a poke in the eye to those who wanted to declare white supremacy dead. How can we know if that's true? Well, what did they say at the time? To go back to our specific example, what were the sentiments expressed when Silent Sam was first unveiled in 1913?

Much like the ill-fated speech for the America First Committee by Charles Lindbergh, the speech given at Silent Sam's unveiling by Julian Carr, a UNC trustee and Civil War veteran, did the statue no favors, although Carr's speech was cheered by the audience, while Lindbergh's audience booed. After wistfully remarking that the Confederate soldiers "saved the very life of the Anglo-Saxon race in the South," Carr rejoiced that on that day in 1913 "the purest strain of the Anglo-Saxon can be found in the 13 Southern States— Praise God." Recalling his Civil War service, Carr then proceeded to share an anecdote with the new graduates regarding an event that he said occurred upon his return from Appomattox, just feet from where he currently stood.

"Silent Sam" statue of Confederate soldier toppled at University of North Carolina, Chapel Hill

I horse-whipped a negro wench until her skirts hung in shreds, because upon the streets of this quiet village she had publicly insulted and maligned a Southern lady, and then rushed for protection to these University buildings where was stationed a garrison of 100 Federal soldiers. I performed the pleasing duty in the immediate presence of the entire garrison, and for thirty nights afterward slept with a double-barrel shotgun under my head.[70]

Equally problematic for Silent Sam but not as well known was that, in the same year the statue was dedicated, the United Daughters of the Confederacy promoted and unanimously endorsed a history of the Ku Klux Klan, noting the heroic work they did to preserve white supremacy.

There have been protests demanding the removal of Silent Sam going back to 1955, and the statue was defaced following the assassination of Martin Luther King Jr. in 1968. Protests continued in later years with many agreeing with UNC history professor Gerald Horne, who wrote in the school paper, "We were always told you can't topple statues because it's akin to toppling history. But monuments are erected to propagandize ideas. They're not just random pieces of furniture." In the 2017–18 academic year, the university spent $390,000 just on cleaning and security for the statue. Finally, on the night before classes began in August 2018, student protesters toppled Silent Sam. The tall monument base remained where it was, but the broken Silent Sam figure was put in a wheelbarrow and taken to an undisclosed location for safekeeping as the university tried to decide what to do.

The UNC chancellor, Carol L. Folt, was in the crosshairs as she tried to work with the university's trustees and board of governors. In December of 2018, the trustees proposed a new "University History and Education Center" on campus with a $5.3 million price tag. The UNC faculty rose up and refused to issue grades at the end of the semester unless the plan to keep Silent Sam anywhere on campus was scrapped.[71] The board of governors formally rejected the plan for the new center, the students got their grades, and, on

---

70   Julian S. Carr, "Unveiling of Confederate Monument at University. June 2, 1913" in the Julian Shakespeare Carr Papers #141, Southern Historical Collection, The Wilson Library, University of North Carolina at Chapel Hill, http://hgreen.people.ua.edu/transcription-carr-speech.html.

71   Joe Killian, "UNC Faculty, Teaching Assistants Withhold Final Grades Over Return of 'Silent Sam,'" NC Policy Watch, December 7, 2018, http://pulse.ncpolicywatch.org/2018/12/07/faculty-teaching-assistants-withhold-grades-at-unc-over-return-of-silent-sam.

January 14, 2019, the pedestal and inscription plaques were removed. The chancellor issued a letter in support of the removal on grounds of public safety; then she resigned. As of this writing the trustees have missed two deadlines for coming up with a new plan with no new deadline announced. It appears that Silent Sam also will be Hidden Sam for the foreseeable future.

Silent Sam is just the latest in a series of Confederate monuments that have been removed either by force or by legislation since 2017. While we argue about it here in the United States, we aren't the only nation to confront the issue of divisive monuments. On April 9, 2003, Iraqis famously pulled down the statue of Saddam Hussein in Baghdad, aided by the U.S. Marines after they took the city at the start of the Iraq war. And then there was Germany after World War II. According to an article in *Politico*,

> In 1949, the Federal Republic of Germany (West Germany) criminalized the display of swastikas; the symbol was also scraped and sometimes blown off of buildings. The federal state systematically destroyed statues and monuments, razed many Nazi architectural structures and buried executed military and civilian officials in mass, unmarked graves so that their resting grounds would not become Nazi shrines.[72]

Back in 1991, as the old Soviet Union fell after the reforms of President Mikhail Gorbachev, the people of Moscow, in a crowd some twenty thousand strong, joyfully destroyed a statue of Felix E. Dzerzhinsky, the father of the Soviet secret police (the KGB). Russian President Boris Yeltsin renamed the plaza "the Square of Free Russia." Many other monuments also were removed and transferred to a section of Muzeon Arts Park, sometimes called the "felled monuments park." In that Moscow park, the description of each monument includes little about the person depicted and each one ends with, "By the decree of the Moscow City Council of people representatives of Oct. 24, 1991, the monument was dismantled and placed in the Muzeon Arts Park exposition. The work is historically and culturally significant, being the memorial construction of the soviet era, on the themes of politics and ideology."[73]

---

72 Joshua Zeitz, "Why There Are No Nazi Statues in Germany: What the South Can Learn from Postwar Europe," *Politico*, August 20, 2017, https://www.politico.com/magazine/story/2017/08/20/why-there-are-no-nazi-statues-in-germany-215510.

73 James Glaser, "What Russia Can Teach the US about What To Do with Confederate Statues after Charlottesville," *Independent*, August 14, 2017, https://www.independent.co.uk/voices/charlottesville-protest-confederate-statue-taken-down-what-to-do-a7892856.html.

More notable is the way many of the statues in the park are placed: sending their own silent message as together they comprise a larger monument that the originals never intended. Some are lined up, intentionally, like tombstones. But there's a lot going on around the large statue of Josef Stalin, under whose rule between fifteen and thirty million people were executed, starved to death, or died in labor camps. Staring up at their tormentor from behind barbed wire and bars are the stone heads of his victims. He faces the other way and cannot see them.

Defaced statue of Josef Stalin and Gulag memorial in Muzeon Arts Park, Moscow

That same article also notes:

> Moreover, in front of Stalin is a contemporary statue of Russian physicist and Nobel Peace Prize winner Andrei Sakharov, one of the most notable dissidents of the Soviet era. The statue of Sakharov is seated, arms behind his back, legs and feet locked together, and head upturned to the sky. Is he staring at the stars, not an unreasonable thing for a scientist or a disarmament activist to do, or can he just not bear to look at Stalin directly in front of him? And what about those arms stretched behind his back, one of them twisted and unnatural, fist in a ball? Is Sakharov being detained, or tortured? That

interpretation is suggested by the statue of Felix Dzerzhinsky, the founder of the KGB, who faces Sakharov about 50 yards away.

In 2012, however, former KGB agent turned Russian president Vladimir Putin began putting statues of Stalin back up outside the park. As of 2017, about ten have gone up in various parts of Russia in a wave of nationalistic fervor and a longing for what Russian nationalists see as the glory days of the old Soviet Union. Putin has condemned the demonization of Stalin as "excessive" and has encouraged a rehabilitation of his image, even hanging a plaque commemorating Stalin in the Moscow State Judicial Academy. A prominent lawyer resigned as a result. Putin's rehabilitation effort appears to be working. A 2017 poll in Russia showed that just 39 percent of Russians believed Stalin's mass repression was a crime, down from 51 percent in 2012. "Repression is a made-up word," said one man. "It was really a fight against crime."[74]

Why do statues go up? Why do they come down? How should we handle a divisive past? More importantly for our purposes, if we apply God's priorities to the question, what might it look like?

Before your next group session, think about the following questions:

- Are monuments a form of speech that should be protected under the First Amendment?

- Is there a difference between UNC students tearing down Silent Sam and Iraqis tearing down the statue of Saddam Hussein?

- Why do you think Confederate statues were put up as late as the 1950s?

- Do the intent and beliefs of those who first erected a monument matter if the monument itself does not articulate them?

- When a symbol has become associated with hate, should it be retired or should there be an attempt to give it a new meaning?

- Who should decide how history is represented? Who should be consulted?

- What is the proper role of museums in this debate?

---

74 Anna Arutunyan, "As Confederate Statues Fall in U.S., Russians Are Erecting Statues for Dictator Stalin," *USA Today*, August 16, 2017, https://www.usatoday.com/story/news/world/2017/08/16/soviet-union-terror-josef-stalin-popularity/556625001.

- Whether you support leaving Confederate monuments alone or whether you want them removed, what does "love your neighbor as yourself" look like from your side?

- Are monuments "graven images"?

CHECK-IN

Write a one-sentence answer to each of the following questions. You will be asked to share these with your group but without further comment:

What is one thing that was new to me in this material?

What is one question that this week's topic(s) raises for me?

ARMED

How to Tame Your Idol

There are just three countries in the world that have a right to bear arms in their constitution: Guatemala, Mexico, and the United States. Other countries allow people to own guns, in varying degrees, but only those three raise weaponry to the level of a constitutional right. Why? And, more importantly for us, are there any idol-related problems with it? Certainly the fruit of the gun debate in the United States has been rotten for quite some time. As with other issues, however, history can give us some perspective and help us to be more informed when we engage the issue and start sniffing about for idols.

THE SECOND AMENDMENT

Amendment II

A well regulated militia, being necessary to the security of a free state, the right of the people to keep and bear arms, shall not be infringed.

Remember back to James Madison writing the Bill of Rights. Madison's original second amendment was slightly different than what Congress finally adopted. His initial language read:

> The right of the people to keep and bear arms shall not be infringed; a well armed and well regulated militia being the best security of a free country: but no person religiously scrupulous of bearing arms shall be compelled to render military service in person.[75]

The religious exemption crafted by Madison was cut in the final version, although the sentiment remained and the right to object to military service on religious grounds was present from the country's founding. But its presence in the first draft makes clear that James Madison's intention with the Second Amendment was to protect the right to bear arms for the purpose of military service rather than for individuals acting on their own. For two centuries, the nation's courts agreed.

Everything in the Constitution was about checks and balances in the government, to ensure that the United States would never find itself with a

---

75   National Constitution Center, "On This Day: James Madison Introduces the Bill of Rights," *Constitution Daily*, June 8, 2018, https://constitutioncenter.org/blog/on-this-day-james-madison-introduces-the-bill-of-rights.

king or other form of autocratic ruler. Congress keeps the president in check, the courts keep Congress in check, the executive branch nominates justices, etc. In addition to the three, co-equal branches of government, there were also checks and balances to allow the states to check the federal government and vice versa. The Second Amendment was one of those. The language about a well-regulated militia was meant to ensure that the states could have a protection force apart from the federal government.

Today we know that force as the National Guard, but in the days after the American Revolution, state militias were more like today's volunteer fire departments—citizens who were willing and able took up arms when the state was threatened, and worked other jobs in the meantime. So it made sense that the federal government should not be able to disarm citizens, since that would put the security of individual states at risk. It was also the case that, with the memory of tyranny fresh in their minds, the founders felt the states needed protection in case tyranny should raise its ugly head in our own federal government. State militias were a must.

Militia interpreters in Colonial Williamsburg

As times and state protection forces changed, there were various cases brought to the Supreme Court. Until the twenty-first century, however, those cases all centered on whether states could have more restrictive gun laws than the federal government (the Court said yes) and whether the right to bear arms applied to individuals or only to state military organizations. The Court repeatedly held that the Second Amendment right did not extend to every individual, but only those who could be construed to be part of that "well regulated militia." The last case in the twentieth century was in 1939, when two men were arrested for carrying a sawed-off shotgun across state lines. The Supreme Court in *U.S. v. Miller* decided:

> In the absence of any evidence tending to show that possession or use of a "shotgun having a barrel of less than eighteen inches in length" at this time has some reasonable relationship to the preservation or efficiency of a well regulated militia, we cannot say that the Second Amendment guarantees the right to keep and bear such an instrument.[76]

That was it until 2008, when there was a handgun ban in Washington, DC, and a licensed special police officer named Dick Heller brought a court challenge to the ban. This time the court saw things differently and in a 5-4 vote ruled:

> The Second Amendment protects an individual right to possess a firearm unconnected with service in a militia, and to use that arm for traditionally lawful purposes, such as self-defense within the home.[77]

While Justice Antonin Scalia's majority opinion opened a number of floodgates, it's worth nothing that even Justice Scalia felt there were limits. In that same opinion he also writes:

> Like most rights, the right secured by the Second Amendment is not unlimited. From Blackstone through the 19th-century cases, commentators and courts routinely explained that the right was not a right to keep and carry any weapon whatsoever in any manner whatsoever and for whatever purpose. . . . [N]othing in our opinion should be taken to cast doubt on longstanding prohibitions on the possession of firearms by felons and the mentally ill, or laws forbidding the carrying of firearms in sensitive places such as schools and government buildings, or laws imposing conditions and qualifications on the commercial sale of arms.

---

76 *United States v. Miller*, 307 U.S. 174 (1939).

77 *District of Columbia v. Heller*, 554 U.S. 570 (2008).

Because the District of Columbia is not a state, it was two more years before another case was brought to have the court decide whether that right to bear arms by individuals not connected to a militia applied also to the states. In another 5-4 ruling, the court said that that right extended to the states as well.

Since those two decisions, the courts have been flooded with gun cases. Just the day after the Heller case was filed, the National Rifle Association brought five lawsuits challenging other local gun bans and there has been no shortage of cases since. There has also been no shortage of shooting deaths.

Gunviolencearchive.org is a nonprofit organization that tracks gun violence statistics. It's a sobering site. I'm writing this sentence on day 147 of 2019. According to gunviolencearchive.org, there have been 147 mass shootings[78] so far this year—one for every day of the year—and 5,618 people killed overall. Another 10,742 have been injured. Of those killed or injured in these first five months, 238 were children under twelve and another 1,056 were teens. In that time 124 law enforcement officers were shot or killed and law enforcement, in turn, shot or killed 804 suspects. There were 581 unintentional shootings.

We're told we need guns to protect ourselves from terrorists, but a 2016 report showed that between 2001 and 2014 the U.S. lost 3,412 people to terrorists either at home or abroad (all but 422 of those were on 9/11) while we lost 440,095 people to gun violence just here on U.S. soil.[79] But while you're looking for terrorists, don't neglect the toddlers. Since 2015, children under the age of four have, on average, shot either themselves or someone else every single week.[80] Think you're safe because you don't have children? Between 2004 and January 2019 at least fifteen of us have been shot by dogs[81], not to mention the Michigan man who was cooking in his kitchen when he was shot by his cat.[82] Have the tuna ready more quickly, people.

---

78   Defined as four or more people shot and killed, not including the shooter.

79   Eve Bower, "American Deaths in Terrorism vs. Gun Violence in One Graph," CNN Online, October 3, 2016, https://www.cnn.com/2016/10/03/us/terrorism-gun-violence/index.html.

80   Walter Einenkel, "For the Last 3 Years, Toddlers Have Been Shooting Themselves and Others on a Weekly Basis," *Daily Kos*, June 9, 2018, https://www.alternet.org/2018/06/last-3-years-toddlers-have-been-shooting-themselves-and-others-weekly-basis.

81   Brian Broom, "Dogs Shooting Humans on Hunting Trips? It's Rare, but It Happens," *Mississippi Clarion Ledger*, January 11, 2019, https://www.clarionledger.com/story/sports/outdoors/2019/01/11/dogs-shoot-hunters-its-rare-but-happens-us-miss/2546121002.

82   Associated Press, "Cat Shoots Owner With 9mm Handgun," Fox News Online, March 10, 2005, https://www.foxnews.com/story/cat-shoots-owner-with-9mm-handgun.

The carnage is as obvious as it is horrifying, and yet any progress toward curbing it is stalled. So what's the problem? If you listen to talk radio or cable news or social media, you would think the nation is sharply divided on what to do. And you would be wrong. The following statistics on gun-related issues come from an Ipsos/Reuters poll conducted from January 11–28, 2019.[83]

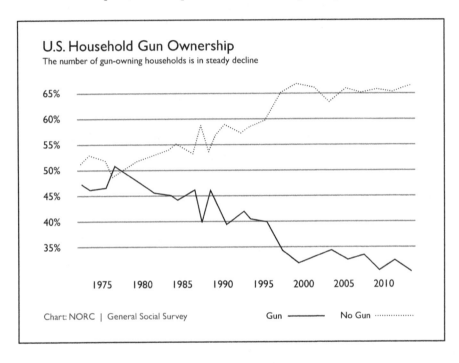

The first thing that stands out in the poll is that, while we seem to hear about guns constantly, only 28 percent of U.S. households have one. When asked about general restrictions on gun ownership, only 7 percent of us believe there should be no or very few restrictions. Here are some policies from that poll that have significant majority support:

People in the U.S. Who Favor. . .

Expanding background checks	84%
Banning military-style assault weapons	69%
Banning semi-automatic weapons	62%

83   Ipsos Poll Conducted for Reuters, "Gun Violence and Gun Laws," February 8, 2019, https://www.ipsos. com/sites/default/files/ct/news/documents/2019-02/2019_reuters_tracking_-_guns_topline_2.8.2019.pdf.

Banning high-capacity ammunition clips	70%
Banning online sales of ammunition	64%
Placing armed security guards in schools	71%
Banning people with mental illness from buying guns	86%
Tracking gun sales through a federal database	80%
Prohibiting people on the no-fly list from buying guns	84%
Raising the legal age to buy a gun from 18 to 21	71%

And there's one last question from that poll that is quite telling. "How confident are you that your elected representatives will do something this year to improve gun laws in the U.S.?" Only 27 percent felt any level of confidence at all.

So what's going on? All it took was one man trying to blow up an airplane with a device in his shoe and for over fifteen years we've all had to take our shoes off to get on an airplane. The Shoe Bomber didn't even succeed and regulations changed almost overnight. Just like the days when the tobacco industry blocked progress on smoking legislation, we now have stalled progress on a life and death issue and bad fruit rotting to high heaven. We know what that means. Something is exerting an outsized influence to make us seem more divided than we really are and to block even the most reasonable solutions. Oh, look! Here's a curtain to pull.

THE NATIONAL RIFLE ASSOCIATION

The National Rifle Association was modeled in part after its British counterpart, and the idea for forming it came from U.S. citizens living in Britain a few months after the Civil War began. They dreamt of an organization that would have shooting competitions and training activities. On November 16, 1871, they got their wish, and the NRA was chartered in New York. The group's first president was Union army general Ambrose Burnside.

General Burnside knew the need for rifle training and practice. Although the Union won the war, it wasn't because of their crackerjack shooting skills. Union army records show it took a thousand shots for every hit. As Burnside himself noted, "Out of ten soldiers who are perfect in drill and the manual of arms, only one knows the purpose of the sights on his gun or can hit the broad side of a barn."[84] Ouch. A site for long-range shooting competitions was built at Creedmoor, Long Island. It paid off. Just two years later, in 1873, when the Irish Rifle Association challenged the U.S. to a competition, the U.S. won and the NRA found itself in the national spotlight for the first time. They organized chapters in other states, where the National Guard often sought their advice and training. In 1907 the NRA moved its headquarters to Washington, DC.

In 1934 the first gun control legislation was proposed in Congress: the National Firearms Act.[85] Gun-related crimes were on the rise and Congress sought to address this by taxing the burgeoning business of manufacturing, importing, and dealing in the specific guns and related accessories targeted in the Act. It also required those firearms to be registered. The $200 tax they imposed was quite severe for the time, though it has not changed since then. Now that it was situated in Washington, the NRA became directly involved in lobbying legislators about this gun control regulation. Here's what NRA president Karl Frederick said in a congressional hearing about the proposed legislation: "I have never believed in the general practice of carrying weapons. I seldom carry one . . . . I do not believe in the general promiscuous toting of guns. I think it should be sharply restricted and only under licenses."[86] The legislation passed with NRA support as did the Federal Firearms Act of 1938 and the Gun Control Act of 1968.

Those laws created a system for the federal licensing of gun dealers and restricted certain kinds of firearms. The NRA used its physical proximity to the legislature in Washington to lobby for its interests, and its power grew. There were some tensions within the organization over whether its original

---

84   David Cole, *Engines of Liberty: How Citizen Movements Succeed* (New York: Basic Books, 2017), 100.

85   Wikipedia, s.v. "National Firearms Act," last modified May 8, 2019, https://en.wikipedia.org/wiki/National_Firearms_Act.

86   Michael S. Rosenwald, "The NRA Once Believed in Gun Control and Had a Leader Who Pushed for It," *Washington Post*, February 22, 2018, https://www.washingtonpost.com/news/retropolis/wp/2017/10/05/the-forgotten-nra-leader-who-despised-the-promiscuous-toting-of-guns.

1934 National Firearms Act

- Brought about by the lawlessness and rise of gangster culture during prohibition
- President Franklin D. Roosevelt hoped this act would eliminate automatic-fire weapons
- Also targeted:
  - Short-barreled shotguns and rifles
  - Parts of guns like silencers
  - "Gadget-style" firearms hidden in canes or pens
- A $200 fine for anyone caught selling or manufacturing these
  - Equivalent to 5 months salary then or $12,525.00 today

mission was being overshadowed, but it wasn't until the mid-1970s that the tensions became an all-out war between those who viewed the organization's mission as promoting sport and training and those who wanted more political engagement and the expansion of gun rights.

Remember that it's important to ask not only, "Why is this happening?" but also, "Why is this happening *now*?" What changed in the 1970s? It's hard to say for certain, but the 1960s saw gun violence bring a nation to its knees in three high-profile assassinations: President John F. Kennedy on November 22, 1963, Rev. Martin Luther King, Jr. on April 4, 1968, and Senator Robert F. Kennedy just two months later, on June 5, 1968. Those killings, combined with the social unrest over racial issues, women's rights, and the war in Vietnam, led to the Gun Control Act of 1968, which passed Congress with the support, if not quite wholehearted, of the NRA.

Then on May 16, 1972, segregationist presidential candidate George Wallace was shot and paralyzed. In the wake of that shooting, President Nixon called for a ban on "Saturday night specials," the cheap and popular small-caliber handguns. As the tapes from Nixon's Oval Office conversations would later reveal, Nixon actually wanted to go further, saying the day after the Wallace shooting,

"I don't know why any individual should have a right to have a revolver in his house. The kids usually kill themselves with it and so forth." He asked his aides why they couldn't go after all handguns. He acknowledged that the NRA and gun manufacturers would be against it, but said simply, "people should not have handguns."[87]

Talked out of it by his aides, Nixon never publicly called for a total ban and the Saturday night special measure never even made it to his desk. Then came the total disruption of the nation that was Watergate with the exposure of the deep corruption in the center of power that resulted in the resignation of both Vice President Spiro Agnew and, of course, President Nixon himself in August 1974.

A NEW SHERIFF IN TOWN

Into societal upheaval, distrust of government, assassinations, corruption, and talk of total gun bans walked an attorney named Harlon Carter, who quickly became the head of the NRA lobbying arm, the Institute for Legislative Action (ILA). When anxiety is high and the foundations of government are shaken, the character of a leader can determine whether unity or division will win the day. So, hold that spot in NRA history as we take a closer look at the man who appears largely responsible for creating the NRA as we know it today.

Born in 1913 in Granbury, Texas, Harlon Carter was the son of an officer in the newly minted United States Border Patrol. When young Harlon was seventeen, someone stole the Carter family's car. Several weeks later, Mrs. Carter said to her son that she suspected some Mexican-American teens who lived near their Laredo home were responsible. Harlon grabbed his gun, found them at a nearby swimming hole, and at gunpoint tried to force them to come home with him. Fifteen-year-old Ramon Casiano resisted and flashed a pocket knife. Harlon shot him dead. Carter was tried and convicted of murder and sentenced to three years in prison, although his conviction was overturned on a technicality after serving only two.

After his release and with a technically clean record, Harlon Carter followed in his father's footsteps and got a job with Border Patrol, rising to lead the patrol from 1950 to 1957. He then moved to the Southwestern Region of

---

87   Associated Press, "Gun Control: Richard Nixon Wished for Total Handgun Ban," *Politico*, March 11, 2013, https://www.politico.com/story/2013/03/gun-control-richard-nixon-wished-for-total-handgun-ban-088686.

Harlon Bronson Carter, 1913-1991, photo by Michael Arthur Worden Evans, c. 1984

The story of Ramon Casiano's murder, along with Carter's subsequent career with Border Patrol and the Southwestern Region of the Immigration and Naturalization Service, was the subject of a 2016 song by a band called Drive-By Truckers, named for Carter's young victim. "Bullet" was a nickname for Carter because of his "bullet" or shaved head.

"Ramon Casiano"

Verse 1

It all started with the border
And that's still where it is today
Someone killed Ramon Casiano
And the killer got away

Down by the Sister Cities river
Two boys with way more pride than sense
One would fall and one would prosper
Never forced to make amends

Verse 2

He became a border agent
And supplemented what he made
With creative deportation
And missing ammo by the case

Since Bullet ran the operation
There's hardly been a minute since
There ain't a massing at the border
From Chinese troops to terrorists

Chorus

He had the makings of a leader
Of a certain kind of man
Who need to feel the world's against him
Out to get 'em if it can

Men whose trigger pull their fingers
Of men who'd rather fight than win
United in a revolution
Like in mind and like in skin

Verse 3

It all started with the border
And that's still where it is today
Down by the Sister Cities river
But for sure no one can say

The killing's been the bullet's business
Since back in 1931
Someone killed Ramon Casiano
And Ramon still ain't dead enough [88]

---

88   Mike Cooley/DBT, copyright Cheap Labor (BMI). Track 1 on the album *American Band*, **ATO Records**, released September 30, 2016. Used with permission.

the Immigration and Naturalization Service, which he led from 1961 to 1970. Harlon Carter's time at our southern border has an eerie resonance. In 1953 he sent a proposal to Washington to have the U.S. military deployed to help Border Patrol conduct "the biggest drive against illegal aliens in history," calling it "Operation Cloudburst." Eisenhower would not support sending troops, but he did appoint a former military general, Joseph Swing, to head INS, and in 1954 Carter joined forces with Swing and the U.S. attorney general to wage "all-out war to hurl . . . Mexican wetbacks back to Mexico." The new name was "Operation Wetback."[89] With that history, let's head back to our NRA timeline in the mid 1970s, with Nixon gone and Harlon Carter out of patrolling the border and instead heading up the lobbying arm of the NRA.

The NRA leadership wanted the organization to return to its sporting and rifle-training roots and leave politics aside. So they proposed moving the NRA from Washington, DC, to Colorado. Carter and the ILA strenuously objected, but the sportsman faction was in leadership and wrested control. On a single weekend in November 1976, the entire staff of the ILA was fired, including Carter and eighty others. Those workers did, however, retain their membership in the NRA and began looking for a way to take control back from the sportsmen and remake the NRA.

Carter teamed up with a gun magazine editor and Christian conservative named Clifford Neal Knox, who was known for suggesting that the assassinations of the 1960s were really a liberal plot to enact gun control legislation. After scouring the NRA bylaws for loopholes, Carter and Knox made their move at the 1977 NRA convention in what would be called "the Revolt at Cincinnati." The old guard was voted out and Harlon Carter was voted in as the NRA's executive vice president—essentially the operative head. Knox took Carter's old job as head of lobbying. From that point forward, the NRA was, at its core, a hardline political operation. In the 1980 election they threw their support to Reagan, who opposed gun restrictions. Harlon Carter's message to Congress was simple: "No compromise, no gun legislation."[90]

---

89   Laura Smith, "The Man Responsible for the Modern NRA Killed a Hispanic Teenager, Before Becoming a Border Agent," *Timeline*, July 6, 2017, https://timeline.com/harlon-carter-nra-murder-2f8227f2434f.

90   Joel Achenbach, Scott Higham, and Sari Horwitz, "How NRA's True Believers Converted a Marksmanship Group into a Mighty Gun Lobby," *Washington Post*, January, 12, 2013, https://www.washingtonpost.com/politics/how-nras-true-believers-converted-a-marksmanship-group-into-a-mighty-gun-lobby/2013/01/12/51c62288-59b9-11e2-88d0-c4cf65c3ad15_story.html.

A 2017 article by Laura Smith describes Carter's time at the NRA this way:

> Carter's tenure was marked by categorical opposition to gun control. When asked if he would "rather allow those convicted violent felons, mentally deranged people, violently addicted to narcotics people to have guns, rather than to have the screening process," he replied that this was the "price we pay for freedom." He advocated for children having the right to possess small pistols, citing a story of a boy who had successfully defended himself from "four bushy guys." *The American Rifleman*, the NRA's magazine, became the voice against gun control. In the years he was in charge, NRA membership tripled.[91]

Carter died in 1991 and Knox in 2005. We will visit with Harlon Carter again when we look at immigration issues in a later volume of this series, but the NRA of the late twentieth and early twenty-first centuries clearly reflects his influence, including the merger of gun interests with conservative Christianity in the person of Neal Knox.

FROM MOSES TO THE GOLDEN CALF

The most famous person associated with the modern NRA was Hollywood actor Charlton Heston, who, ironically for our purposes here, played Moses in the Cecil B. deMille classic film *The Ten Commandments*. Heston was president of the NRA from 1998 until 2003, beating out Neal Knox by a scant four votes. While the position of NRA president is largely ceremonial, he quickly became its face. As the 2000 campaign between George W. Bush and Al Gore heated up, the NRA sided with Bush. At the NRA annual meeting that year, Heston used religious imagery as he spoke of the "sacred stuff" that "resides in that wooden stock and blued steel." He then made the following appeal: "As we set out this year to defeat the divisive forces that would take freedom away, I want to say those fighting words for everyone within the sound of my voice to hear and to heed—and especially for you, Mr. Gore—" he then lifted the replica of a Colonial musket he was holding and said, "from my cold, dead hands!"[92] Just those few sentences made my idolspotting radar explode.

---

91   Smith, "The Man Responsible for the Modern NRA."

92   Achenbach, "How NRA's True Believers . . . "

NRA President Charlton Heston holds up a rifle as he addresses gun owners during a "get-out—the-vote" rally in Manchester, NH, October 21, 2002

Wayne LaPierre was a one-time legislative aide and NRA member that Knox had recruited to his lobbying group in 1978. LaPierre became the NRA executive vice president in 1991. That was the position Harlon Carter had held, and that is where the real power of the organization lies. LaPierre remains in that position today, barely surviving an attempt to oust him at the NRA annual meeting in April 2019. He earns about one million dollars a year, plus speaking fees and royalties from book sales, and his lavish spending on clothing and travel remain under internal investigation.[93] Under his leadership, the organization has moved further and further to the right, eventually refusing to even speak with related government agencies like the Bureau of Alcohol, Tobacco, and Firearms. Like with Carter, it is all or nothing with LaPierre, who said at the 2002 annual meeting, "We must declare that there are no shades of gray in American freedom. It's black and white, all or nothing."[94]

The NRA has endowed the Patrick Henry Professorship of Constitutional Law and the Second Amendment at George Mason University, publishes a variety of

---

93 Tim Mak, "As Leaks Show Lavish NRA Spending, Former Staff Detail Poor Conditions at Nonprofit," *npr*, May 15, 2019, https://www.npr.org/2019/05/15/722960414/as-leaks-show-lavish-nra-spending-former-staff-detail-poor-conditions-at-nonprof.

94 Achenbach: "How NRA's True Believers . . ."

newsletters and glossy magazines, hosts a weekly TV show, a satellite news service, and of course a robust website and social media presence. The organization even has its own museum. In 2016, the NRA spent $419 million[95], hiked its membership fees for the first time in twenty years, and boasted an increase in membership. And yet, despite an increased membership paying higher fees, their financial records for 2017 showed a 22 percent drop in membership revenue. Media outlets began to examine their funding and discovered millions in debt.[96] Perhaps the organization was not as strong as it seemed.

On Valentine's Day 2018, a teen gunman with a semi-automatic rifle shot and killed seventeen students and teachers and wounded fourteen others at Marjory Stoneman Douglas High School in Parkland, Florida. It wasn't the first school shooting by any means, nor was it the last. But after decades of inaction despite calls from a wide majority for change, the survivors at Parkland decided they'd had enough.

The Parkland students were old enough, bold enough, and came from a privileged enough community to mount a national campaign called March for Our Lives. Just five weeks after the shooting, they had raised millions of dollars and gathered an estimated two hundred thousand people for a rally in Washington, DC. When school let out, they spent their summer vacation on a bus tour of the country to push for gun reform legislation and to register young people to vote in the 2018 midterm elections. And they pointed their young, bold fingers at the NRA, the force they believed was largely responsible for blocking any solution to the problem of gun violence.

95   Nick Wing, "NRA Spending Approached Half a Billion Dollars in 2016," *Huffington Post*, November 16, 2017, https://www.huffpost.com/entry/nra-2016-spending_n_5a0dd3e6e4b0b17e5e14e636.

96   John Cook, "NRA Membership Dues Tumbled Last Year," *The Trace*, September 20, 2018, https://www. thetrace.org/2018/09/nra-membership-dues-decline-2017.

Much of the public was with the students, and Harlon Carter's old mantra of, "No compromise. No gun legislation," showed signs of strain. The NRA responded to Parkland with an urgent call for new members, producing a brief membership spike and influx of funding. They hiked their dues again in 2018. But the tide was turning. In the wake of the Parkland shooting and the March for Our Lives, fifty new gun-control laws were passed in state legislatures, including fourteen with Republican governors. The Trump Administration banned bump stocks in December 2018. Retailers, including Dick's Sporting Goods and Walmart, began to limit gun sales, and financial institutions like Bank of America and Citigroup began to limit the financing of firearms.

As the built-up sentiment on the outside was storming the NRA gates, the U.S. Department of Justice was pulling back the curtain and exposing at least one voice behind the microphone. On July 16, 2018, the U.S. Department of Justice announced their indictment of Maria Butina, a twenty-nine-year-old Russian gun rights activist who later pled guilty to failing to register as a Russian agent within the U.S.[97] Her Russian mentor and lifetime NRA member, Alexander Torshin, brought Butina to the NRA convention in 2014, where she mingled with leadership, including Wayne LaPierre, and important members. In successive years the NRA connection to evangelical Christianity, begun by Clifford Neal Knox, allowed her to waltz easily into conservative political and religious circles where she sought out influential leaders. Both Torshin and Butina have regularly attended the National Prayer Breakfast in Washington, DC.[98]

Maria Butina in Moscow in a photo she posted to Facebook in October 2013

---

97 As of this writing Maria Butina is serving an eighteen-month sentence, given considerable leniency by the prosecution after she gave investigators substantial assistance about related cases.

98 Katherine Stewart, "What Was Maria Butina Doing at the National Prayer Breakfast?" *New York Times*, July 18, 2018, https://www.nytimes.com/2018/07/18/opinion/maria-butina-putin-infiltration.html.

Alexander Torshin, with ties to the Russian government, is a senior official at the Russian Central Bank and was sanctioned by the U.S. government in 2018. The NRA is a tax-exempt nonprofit organization and as of this writing is under FBI investigation for money laundering. Since they are still chartered in New York, the New York attorney general also has opened an investigation into their tax-exempt status and has subpoenaed some of their related organizations. With accusations about financial misconduct flying, NRA president Oliver North attempted to oust Wayne LaPierre at the 2019 annual meeting. Instead it was North who ended up resigning, after only one year at the helm.[99]

While the outcome of all those investigations has not been determined as of this writing, the gradual movement toward gun reform legislation and the myriad legal woes of the NRA may indicate that an idol is being exposed. There have been more U.S. citizens killed by guns since 1968 than in all U.S. wars.[100] Was Harlon Carter right? Is that really the price we have to pay for this particular freedom? Or did idols betray us for thirty pieces of silver? Perhaps the Second Amendment will soon have an opening to return to its important role within, rather than above, the checks and balances of the United States Constitution.

DUPED INTO DIVISION

While the majority favor gun regulations and restrictions, we should always be careful with "majority rule." For a long time the majority wanted slavery, after all. When a minority group claims they are being harmed, the majority has a responsibility to listen and to see if there is merit to the claim. This is true for all of us, but is especially true for Christians. We have pledged to follow the guy who loved, blessed, and cared for marginalized people and who charged those in power to do the same. So when a minority of people cry out that their rights are being infringed, whether it's gun rights or anything else, we have an obligation to listen. The vision of justice we longed for in chapter one isn't just for the majority. It's for everyone.

---

99 Danny Hakim, "N.R.A. President to Step Down as New York Attorney General Investigates," *New York Times*, April 27, 2019, https://www.nytimes.com/2019/04/27/us/oliver-north-nra.html.

100 Nicholas Kristof, "Lessons from the Virginia Shooting," *New York Times*, August 26, 2015, https://www.nytimes.com/2015/08/27/opinion/lessons-from-the-murders-of-tv-journalists-in-the-virginia-shooting.html.

But to have a debate and come to a lasting resolution, we have to speak with real people and hear their real concerns. With millions doing that speaking and listening on social media, we are open to manipulation in ways and on a scale that weren't possible before such platforms gained wide use. In 2018, sixty-eight percent of people in the U.S. reported getting at least part of their news from social media sites, with four in ten getting it from Facebook.[101] Why get our news there? Because we trust our friends to give it to us straight. But should we?

In the fourth quarter of 2018, Facebook estimated that there were 116 million fake accounts on its platform.[102] Many thought that number was actually much higher, and they were right. Between January and March of 2019, Facebook removed 2.2 billion fake accounts and changed their number for the previous quarter to 1.2 billion. That's a lot when you consider Facebook has 2.38 billion monthly active users.[103] Twitter suspended more than 70 million fake accounts in May and June of 2018 alone,[104] and many believe that figure is also much lower than the reality. Fake accounts on both platforms were tied to Russia, Venezuela, and Iran, among others.[105]

Many of those accounts wanted to scam people out of money by selling fake goods or trying to get donations for a bogus cause. But a lot of others were set up very specifically to tear the scab off of our national wounds and to weaponize the strengths of our First Amendment freedoms against us. Hostile nations see no need to send an invading army if a small investment in online bots and trolls can convince us to fight and destroy ourselves.

101 Katerina Eva Matsa and Elisa Shearer, "News Use Across Social Media Platforms 2018," Pew Research Center, September 10, 2018, https://www.journalism.org/2018/09/10/news-use-across-social-media-platforms-2018.

102 Jack Nicas, "Does Facebook Really Know How Many Fake Accounts It Has?" *New York Times*, January 30, 2019, https://www.nytimes.com/2019/01/30/technology/facebook-fake-accounts.html.

103 Kaya Yurieff, "Facebook Removed 2.2 Billion Fake Accounts in Three Months," May 23, 2019, https://www.cnn.com/2019/05/23/tech/facebook-transparency-report/index.html.

104 Craig Timberg and Elizabeth Dwoskin, "Twitter Is Sweeping Out Fake Accounts Like Never Before, Putting User Growth at Risk," *Washington Post*, July 6, 2018, https://www.washingtonpost.com/technology/2018/07/06/twitter-is-sweeping-out-fake-accounts-like-never-before-putting-user-growth-risk.

105 Donie O'Sullivan, "Facebook and Twitter Remove Thousands of Fake Accounts Tied to Russia, Venezuela and Iran," CNN Business, January. 31, 2019, https://www.cnn.com/2019/01/31/tech/twitter-facebook-account-suspensions/index.html.

> **Hostile nations see no need to send an invading army if a small investment in online bots and trolls can convince us to fight and destroy ourselves.**

The rules of the idol game are as old as the hills, and we've learned to spot them, but the methods they employ are ever new and changing. All they need is an opening to exploit. Our online conversations about issues that trouble us where bad actors can pretend to be what they are not is fertile ground, especially when combined with the stresses and anxieties of today's world.

We are in the midst of an enormous societal shift not seen since the Industrial Revolution. Technology has made our lives both infinitely more manageable and more dangerous. Drones can drop packages or bombs. Your smart-home gadgets can provide enormous convenience, both for you and for hackers, who can harness the signals from all those devices to flood and crash internet providers, bringing the economy to a standstill. Technology that makes things easier and cheaper also puts people out of work as entire industries go the way of carriage makers and blacksmiths.

Changes to the climate add to those anxieties with natural disasters, more severe weather, and exacerbating disease and conflict over diminishing resources. The entire world is on edge as governments of all kinds struggle to find ways to stabilize their economies and care for their people. The Maldives Archipelago has bought land in Australia as they prepare for a mass migration to move their entire country, which is expected to be entirely underwater within the next thirty years.[106] Indonesia is trying to move its capital of Jakarta, which is sinking faster than any other city in the world. In ten years, half of the city of ten million people could be under water.[107] Countries like Syria, who were already at the edge, have fallen prey to the idols of cruel dictators and terrorists waiting in the wings, and their refugees swamp their neighbors.

Such conditions can provide the opening that idols crave. We have seen how similar upheavals in times past have caused divisions that are very similar

---

106 James Burgess, "Maldives Buying Land in Australia as Preparation for Mass Migration." OilPrice.com, January 10, 2012, https://oilprice.com/Latest-Energy-News/World-News/Maldives-Buying-Land-In-Australia-As-Preparation-For-Mass-Migration.html.

107 Linda Poon, "Why Indonesia Wants to Move Its Capital Out of Jakarta," *Citylab*, May 6, 2019, https://www.citylab.com/environment/2019/05/indonesia-moving-capital-sink-jakarta-jokowi-climate-change/588415.

to our own. But while the divisions have familiar themes, today's idols have powerful new tools at their disposal and those tools are developing so quickly that it can be hard to keep up. Here's one example of how fake social media accounts are being used to make us appear to be more divided than we are.

A Facebook group called "Heart of Texas" organized a rally to "Stop Islamization of Texas." The rally date was set for noon on May 21, 2016, outside of an Islamic center in Houston. Hundreds of thousands joined the group on Facebook. Another Facebook group, "Save Islamic Knowledge," organized a counter-protest for the same time and place. When the day came, both groups showed up and the confrontation was heated, with Texans on both sides hurling hate and provoking skirmishes.

Protesters and counter protesters at the Heart of Texas Rally outside the Islamic Da'wah Center in Houston, Texas

When Facebook released to Congress the first set of fake Russian pages designed to influence the 2016 election, their data showed that both Heart of Texas and Save Islamic Knowledge were set up and run by Russians who had paid people to sow discord. They organized online and duped hundreds of thousands of real Texans into supporting one side or the other. Then their paid protestors—some with Heart of Texas and others with Save Islamic Knowledge—showed up to make sure their unwitting participants were goaded into as ugly a confrontation as possible.[108]

---

108 Claire Albright, "A Russian Facebook Page Organized a Protest in Texas. A Different Russian Page Launched the Counterprotest," *The Texas Tribune*, November 1, 2017, https://www.texastribune.org/2017/11/01/russian-facebook-page-organized-protest-texas-different-russian-page-l.

It started online but moved into the real streets of Houston, where the media naturally covered it, magnifying the discord and enraging people across the country who otherwise would have had no idea it even happened. Some who previously might have wanted to discuss concerns on either side looked at the ugliness and said, "I can't believe how horrible they are!" and came away believing their own side was in the right because—well—look what they were saying! Good people don't act like that! An already difficult issue—understanding between religions and anxiety over changing demographics—was scooped up by the Russians in order to make sure the existing wedge went even deeper, lessening the chance of healing. Their hope was—and still is—that offensive behavior and the dangers of possible violence would make any would-be peacemakers say, "Well, you certainly can't reason with *those* people." In that way divisions are deepened instead of resolved and the fabric of our democracy, which depends on goodwill, truth, and a desire for unity, is ripped to shreds. The Russians bought the beating heart of Texas for only $200 and sent it into cardiac arrest.

The world is often not as it seems, and at times we feel like we're living in a land of mirrors. While it's understandable that we would be anxious, there's no reason to panic. As long as we can keep calm and remember our priorities, we can pull back the curtain and help everyone to realize that, as powerful as this thing seems—whatever it is—there is One who is more powerful yet. If we hold off on our instinct to punch back for just a moment, we can remember that the one thing more powerful than fear is love. Maybe we can't talk about certain issues with some people for now. Maybe we actually have to be physically separate from a friend or loved one for a time. But don't burn the bridge. "You'll always be precious to me, but I need some time away from this debate to sort out my thoughts," or something like that, can help keep us from permanent breaks we might later regret.

In times like these, we all can be easily fooled. Maybe your loved one has been tricked. Or, maybe it's you. Or maybe it's all of us. Jesus never promised that living a life that put God first would be easy. In Matthew 10:16, he says to his disciples, "See, I am sending you out like sheep into the midst of wolves; so be wise as serpents and innocent as doves." It's good advice.

THERE'S NO PLACE LIKE HOME

The Ten Commandments took a large group of freed Hebrew slaves and turned them into a nation, serving as Israel's constitution in all senses of that word. It was that agreement to love God by acting justly toward each other that allowed them to leave the desert and enter the promised land. Every time they stumbled, that home was in jeopardy. At times, the Bible tells us, it was actually lost. We face the same risk.

Like the Constitution of the United States, the Ten Commandments leave lots of room for interpretation and refinement. The ancient Israelites developed their own system for clarifying their meaning, just as we have done for our own governing principles. But the only way any such principles produce justice and create the home for which we long is if we pay attention, centering our priorities not just in our minds but in our lives. Merely affirming a set of priorities doesn't turn hell into heaven. To inhabit a world filled with the fruit that will heal the nations, our priorities need not just to be affirmed, but practiced.

A man in a church I served got up week after week to ask for prayer for a good friend of his who needed a kidney transplant. Again and again he asked us to pray that a donor might be found. One week the man got up again. But this time his request had changed. He told us he had been tested himself and found to be a perfect match. Now he wanted additional prayer for himself as he prepared to donate one of his own kidneys to his friend. "I discovered I was the answer to my prayer," he said. Words don't save the world. Only the word made flesh can do that.

Words don't save the world. Only the word made flesh can do that.

While the later commandments will give more detail, the necessary conditions for all the rest are here at the beginning: No other gods. Keep idols out; and please, for the love of God, don't make any yourselves. If we fail in that, we have taken God's name in vain, we have affirmed God's priorities in vain, and the rest of the commandments will only reap the whirlwind. When we neglect our highest priorities or trade them for a shiny idol, our seeds of justice will produce only a crown of thorns.

But, fear not. We don't have to live with flying monkeys. If we challenge the idol's lie that justice is for some but not others; if we recognize that love of God is made manifest in our love of neighbor; if we change our own behavior before casting judgment on others, we will understand what Jesus meant when he said "For, in fact, the kingdom of God is among you." (Luke 17:21) We don't need to hitch a ride with a would-be wizard from Kansas. The power to go home has always been ours.

- Love the Lord your God with all your heart, and with all your soul, and with all your mind, and love your neighbor as yourself.

- Do justly, love mercy, walk humbly with your God.

- Thou shalt have no other gods before me.

Those are the priorities that result in justice; and it is justice that will lead us home.

Do not be daunted by the enormity of the world's grief.

Do justly now.

Love mercy now.

Walk humbly now.

You are not obligated to complete the work,
but neither are you free to abandon it.[109]

---

109 From Rami Shapiro, *Wisdom of the Jewish Sages: A Modern Reading of Pirke Avot*, 41. Harmony/Bell Tower (March 21, 1995), 160 pages Paraphrase of Rabbi Rami Shapiro's interpretive translation of Rabbi Tarfon's work on the Pirke Avot 2:20. The text is a commentary on Micah 6:8.

PREPARING FOR YOUR FINAL GROUP SESSION

Note ... this is a different set of questions than the other chapters.

CHECK-IN

Write a one-sentence answer to each of the following questions. You will be asked to share these with your group but without further comment:

What is one concern on the other side of the gun debate that I really **can't** understand?

What is one concern on the other side of the gun debate that I really **do** understand?

Reflect on the following questions about your own experiences with guns and gun culture:

- Did you grow up with guns in the house? If so, were they accessible to you? Were you ever trained to use them?

- In your family of origin, what was the attitude toward guns generally? How about in your household now?

- Did you or do you have any important relationships where guns are a point of connection?

- Have you had an experience with gun violence either directly or indirectly?

- When you consider the gun debate, what is one thing you just can't understand about those on the other side?

- Have you ever lost a relationship because of this issue?

- Over the years, has your position on this issue ever shifted? In what way?

- Is owning a gun important to you? Why or why not?

- Why do you think guns are so tied to our national story?

In your group session you'll have an opportunity to share some of your experiences and thoughts about guns. That will not be required, but could be helpful to understanding why people take the positions they do. Consider what you might be willing to share with your group to help that understanding.

Think back over all the reading and group experiences in light of the following questions:

- Did you learn anything new?

- Do you feel any more able to talk about social issues than when you began?

- Has this been a positive or negative experience for you?

- Are there any issues where your position has either softened or shifted one way or another? If so, what do you think caused that change?

- Whatever your position is on an issue discussed in this volume, do you feel better able to understand the position of the other side?

- Do you think people in your group were open and honest with each other about their positions?

- Do you think the reading material presented the issues fairly?

- Are you typically one to share opinions with others or do you usually keep your ideas to yourself? Has that changed any over the course of this study?

- Did you feel unable to express your opinion in the group? If so, was that because of the structured exercises or discussion questions or because of personalities within the group?

You'll see those questions again on an anonymous written evaluation in your final session. You'll be given an envelope so you can seal your responses before giving them back to your leader who will send them in to the Massachusetts Bible Society. We value your feedback and read every word of every evaluation sent to us. Thank you for taking the time.

FURTHER READING

For those who want to explore the topics in this volume more deeply, the following are titles that interesect with one or more of the themes in this volume.

GENERAL BOOKS ON JUSTICE AND LAW

Robert Tsai, *Practical Equality: Forging Justice in a Divided Nation*, W. W. Norton & Company, 2019.

Michael J. Sandel, *Justice: What's the Right Thing to Do?* Farrar, Straus and Giroux, Reprint edition, 2010.

Bryan Stevenson, *Just Mercy: A Story of Justice and Redemption*, Spiegel & Grau, Reprint edition, 2015.

Glenn C. Altschuler and Faust F. Rossi, *Ten Great American Trials: Lessons in Advocacy*, American Bar Association, 2017.

....

PROTEST AND RESISTANCE

Bonnie Siegler, *Signs of Resistance: A Visual History of Protest in America*, Artisan, 2018.

Phil Cushway (Compiler), Michael Warr (Editor), and Victoria Smith

(Photographer), *Of Poetry and Protest: From Emmett Till to Trayvon Martin*, W. W. Norton & Company, 2016.

Ginger Gaines-Cirelli, *Sacred Resistance: A Practical Guide to Christian Witness and Dissent*, Abingdon Press, 2018.

....

CHRISTIANITY AND SOCIAL JUSTICE

Jonathan L. Walton, *A Lens of Love: Reading the Bible in Its World for Our World*, Westminster John Knox Press, 2018.

Walter Brueggemann, *Interrupting Silence: God's Command to Speak Out*, Westminster John Knox Press, 2018.

Vic McCracken (Editor), *Christian Faith and Social Justice: Five Views*, Bloomsbury Academic, 2014.

Eric R. Severson, *Scandalous Obligation: Rethinking Christian Responsibility*, Beacon Hill Press of Kansas City, 2011.

....

NATIONAL SYMBOLS

Tim Marshall, *A Flag Worth Dying For: The Power and Politics of National Symbols*, Politics of Place Series, Book 2, Scribner, 2018.

Marc Ferris, *Star-Spangled Banner: The Unlikely Story of America's National Anthem*, Johns Hopkins University Press, 2014.

Jefferson Morley, *Snow-Storm in August: Washington City, Francis Scott Key, and the Forgotten Race Riot of 1835*, Nan A. Talese/Doubleday, 2012.

Richard J. Ellis, *To the Flag: The Unlikely History of the Pledge of Allegiance*, University Press of Kansas, 2005.

....

EXCEPTIONALISM AND NATIONALISM

John D. Wilsey, *American Exceptionalism and Civil Religion: Reassessing the History of an Idea*, IVP Academic, 2015.

Jeff Sharlet, *The Family: The Secret Fundamentalism at the Heart of American Power*, Harper Perennial, 2009.

Benedict Anderson, *Imagined Communities: Reflections on the Origin and Spread of Nationalism*, Verso, Revised edition, 2016.

John B. Judis, *The Nationalist Revival: Trade, Immigration, and the Revolt Against Globalization*, Columbia Global Reports, 2018.

Michael Ignatieff, *Blood and Belonging: Journeys into the New Nationalism*, Farrar, Straus and Giroux, Reprint edition, 1995.

WHITE SUPREMACY

Eli Saslow, *Rising Out of Hatred: The Awakening of a Former White Nationalist*, Doubleday, 2018.

Kathleen Belew, *Bring the War Home: The White Power Movement and Paramilitary America*, Harvard University Press, 2018.

Henry Louis Gates Jr., *Stony the Road: Reconstruction, White Supremacy, and the Rise of Jim Crow*, Penguin Press, 2019.

CHURCH AND STATE IN THE U.S.

Forrest Church (Editor), *The Separation of Church and State: Writings on a Fundamental Freedom by America's Founders*, Beacon Press, 2011.

David L. Holmes, *The Faiths of the Founding Fathers*, Oxford University Press, 2006.

John M. Barry, *Roger Williams and the Creation of the American Soul: Church, State, and the Birth of Liberty*, Penguin Books, 2012.

Joseph Kip Kosek (Editor), *American Religion, American Politics: An Anthology*, Yale University Press, 2017.

Jeff Sharlet, *The Family: The Secret Fundamentalism at the Heart of American Power*, Harper Perennial, 2009.

Mark A. Noll, *God and Race in American Politics: A Short History*, Princeton University Press, 2010.

HUMAN RIGHTS

Lynn Hunt, *Inventing Human Rights: A History*, W. W. Norton & Company, 2008.

Michael Ignatieff, *Human Rights as Politics and Idolatry, Book 26 of The University Center for Human Values Series*, Princeton University Press, 2003.

Mary Ann Glendon, *A World Made New: Eleanor Roosevelt and the Universal Declaration of Human Rights*, Random House Trade Paperbacks, 2002.

BILL OF RIGHTS

Ellen Alderman and Caroline Kennedy, *In Our Defense: The Bill of Rights in Action*, Avon Books, Reprint edition, 1992.

David Bodenhamer and James W. Ely, Jr. (Editors), *The Bill of Rights in Modern America*, Revised and Expanded, Indiana University Press, 2008.

THE FIRST AMENDMENT

Charles Slack, *Liberty's First Crisis: Adams, Jefferson, and the Misfits Who Saved Free Speech*, Grove Press, 2016.

Floyd Abrams, *The Soul of the First Amendment*, Yale University Press, 2018.

....

THE SECOND AMENDMENT

Patrick J. Charles, *Armed in America: A History of Gun Rights from Colonial Militias to Concealed Carry*, Prometheus Books, 2018.

Michael Waldman, *The Second Amendment: A Biography*, Simon & Schuster, 2015.

Joyce Lee Malcolm, *To Keep and Bear Arms: The Origins of an Anglo-American Right*, Harvard University Press, 1996.

GROUP COVENANT

We covenant together to deal with our differences in a spirit of mutual respect and to refrain from actions that may harm the emotional and physical well-being of others.

The following principles will guide our actions:

- We will treat others whose views may differ from our own with the same courtesy we would want to receive ourselves.

- We will listen with a sincere desire to understand the point of view being expressed by another person, especially if it is different from our own.

- We will respect each other's ideas, feelings, and experiences.

- We will refrain from blaming or judging in our attitude and behavior toward others.

- We will communicate directly with any person with whom we may disagree in a respectful and constructive way.

- We will seek feedback to ensure that we have truly understood each other in our communications.

- We will maintain confidentiality.

FINAL EVALUATION

Church or Group Name

Location   Group Leader

....

Think back over all the reading and group experiences in light of the following questions.

On a scale of 1–10, how much do you agree with the following statements:

1 = Strongly disagree   10 = Strongly agree

....

I learned something new.   _____

I feel more able to talk about social issues than when I began.   _____

This has been a positive experience for me.   _____

I now understand the other side of some issues differently.   _____

Those in my group were open and honest with their opinions.   _____

Those in my group were respectful of one another.   _____

The reading material presented issues fairly.   _____

I typically share my opinions with others.   _____

I enjoyed the exercises in our group sessions.   _____

I felt unable to express my opinions in our group.   _____

The exercises made it safer to express my opinions and ideas.   _____

I enjoyed the reading.   _____

We covered important issues.   _____

Other comments:

_____

_____
_____
_____
_____
_____
_____
_____
_____
_____
_____
_____
_____
_____
_____
_____
_____
_____
_____
_____

Add me to your email list:

ACKNOWLEDGMENTS

This isn't just a book; it's a project and projects take teams of people to create. In this case I'd like to especially thank five teams that have helped to create this first volume of *Exploring Justice: The Ten Commandments*. Here they are in order of appearance:

First is the Board of Trustees of the Massachusetts Bible Society, led by our president, Rev. David Killian. Without a green light from the board, I could not have had the time and resources to write. I thank them for their trust in embarking on a multi-year project to create a vehicle for dialogue about the Bible, social justice, and what the healing of the nations might look like today. I hope this first volume confirms their act of faith.

Books don't publish themselves, however, and all the faith and trust in the world doesn't magically produce the dollars needed to create and promote them. I am grateful to every person who gave to our campaign to raise the production money for this volume. People giving a recurring gift were allowed to dedicate their gift in honor or memory of someone. Nancy Wichmann dedicated her gift in memory of Laura Anne Wichmann and Joyce Simon dedicated her gift in memory of Rev. Jack R. Stevens.

Once I start work on a project like this, greater burdens are placed on the MBS staff. There are permissions for quoted text and images to be obtained, communications to be drafted, promotions to be planned, and more general work that has to be picked up while I devote myself to writing. When things slide off my plate, Mike Colyott and Pamela Piliero are there to catch them and make sure that everything still functions smoothly and that we have what we need when we need it. They are invaluable.

All of our study materials are tested in local churches, even before they go through the editing process. Working only with very rough drafts, these pilot congregations gather a group to do the entire six-week study and provide detailed feedback on their experience every week. The following is a list of the six pilot congregations and their group leaders who tested this volume:

- Christ Lutheran Church in Natick, MA. Led by Joyce Simon.
- First Unitarian Society of Newton, MA. Led by Barbara Bates.
- St. Peter's Lutheran Church in Harwich, MA. Led by Rev. Christian Holleck.
- The Paulist Center in Boston, MA. Led by Mary Burke.
- Union Church in Waban, MA. Led by Rev. Stacy Swain.
- Waquoit Congregational Church in East Falmouth, MA. Led by Rev. Nell Fields.

To every member of every one of those groups, thank you. As you read the finished volume, you will see just how much your feedback re-shaped that initial draft that you used. And to those doing the study in its finished form, you have no idea how thankful you should be for their help!

The last team to take the baton is the editorial and production team: Nancy Fitzgerald, editor; Jennifer Hackett, copyeditor; Tom Bergeron, designer; and Maria Boyer, proofreader. They make sure the material is as easy to read as it is beautiful to look at. They also make sure I have citations where they are needed, that style guides are both created and followed, and that the final product is worthy of both your purchase and your study. I am grateful that the same team that helped us bring you *Exploring the Bible: The Dickinson Series* was willing to go another round with *Exploring Justice: The Ten Commandments*.

My Notes

My Notes

My Notes

My Notes

My Notes

Made in the USA
Columbia, SC
23 September 2019